Manifestation Pe......

"*Manifestation Perfected* is more than just a guide; it's an invitation to align with your soul's purpose and embrace your highest potential. With his intuitive six-step process, Baptist demystifies the art of manifestation, grounding it in practical spirituality and real-life success stories. This book is a must-read for anyone ready to flow confidently with the universe and create a life they love."

~ **GEORGE LIZOS**, creator of Intuition Mastery School and author of *Ancient Manifestation Secrets* and *Protect Your Light*

"Study this book and learn how you can use this invisible, magical power to create your own future."

~ **MICHAEL PILARCZYK**, founder of Mastermind Academy and author of *Master Your Mindset*

"To me, manifesting is another word for seeing. With your eyes open or closed. Seeing. And then you can—with trial and error—follow this seeing. The success of my magazine *Happinez* is living proof of this. If you want to learn to manifest, this book will be a great signpost."

~ **INEZ vAN OORD**, publisher, writer, and founder of the mindstyle magazine *Happinez*

"In a world full of celebrity gossip and controversy, Baptist cuts through to the heart of the matter: every one of us is a Soul, and we can either recognize that or continue the illusion of struggle. No matter what you read on the online rumor mill, Baptist still sees a Soul in every human being. It's easy to admire his commitment to this simple, timeless truth: we are all One. Baptist is a compassionate and insightful visionary who has the ability to see beyond the veil of illusion no matter what the story is."

- **KURT JOHNSON**, manifestation coach and president of New World Allstar, LLC

MANIFESTATION PERFECTED

Six Steps to Embody
Your Soul Purpose

Baptist de Pape

FINDHORN PRESS

Findhorn Press
One Park Street
Rochester, Vermont 05767
www.findhornpress.com

Findhorn Press is a division of Inner Traditions International

Originally published in Dutch in 2022 by Kosmos Uitgevers as *Leer manifesteren zoals Oprah Winfrey en J.K. Rowling*

English edition published in 2025 by Findhorn Press

Disclaimer
The information in this book is given in good faith and intended for information only. Neither author nor publisher can be held liable by any person for any loss or damage whatsoever which may arise from the use of this book or any of the information therein.

Cataloging-in-Publication data for this title is available from the Library of Congress

ISBN 979-8-88850-251-8 (print)
ISBN 979-8-88850-252-5 (ebook)

Printed and bound in the United States by Lake Book Manufacturing, LLC

10 9 8 7 6 5 4 3 2 1

Edited by Jacqui Lewis
Text design and layout by Yasko Takahashi
This book was typeset in Adobe Garamond Pro and Gill Sans Nova

To send correspondence to the author of this book, mail a first-class letter to the author c/o Inner Traditions • Bear & Company, One Park Street, Rochester, VT 05767, USA and we will forward the communication, or contact the author directly at **baptist@thepoweroftheheart.com**.

Contents

PART THREE

Staying in Alignment with Your Soul

PART FOUR

Identifying the Intentions of Your Soul

PART FIVE

Manifesting from the Intention of the Soul

PART SIX

Our Task Is to Manifest

Preface

You are what your deep, driving desire is. As your desire is, so is your
will. As your will is, so is your deed. As your deed is, so is your destiny.
— Brihadaranyaka Upanishad IV.4.5

Manifesting—the ability to bring things into your world that you
want and need—has three aspects.

The first aspect is purely physical and has been proved in laboratory tests. This form of manifesting is sometimes called optimism,
and what happens is that optimists tend to make better and more
productive choices than pessimists. In fact, some pessimists find it
difficult to make any choices at all, and so remain stuck where they
are. In contrast to this, optimists are more likely to see possibilities
that pessimists miss, and so they bring more good things into their
lives because they take action. And so the optimist will be more likely
to manifest the life he or she can imagine.

The second form of manifesting is also purely physical, and it has
to do with the body's internal chemistry. When we feel an emotion the
body creates a chemical change that affects the brain. If we're frightened the body creates adrenalin, and so we feel the energy attached to
that chemical. The body also produces chemicals when we feel good,
and if we keep feeling upbeat it will continue to supply us with that

same chemical. When we feel upbeat we tend to be optimistic, and so we're much more likely to choose well in our lives. This is a physical fact, and has been measured many times in experimental situations.

The third aspect of manifesting is metaphysical—it's easy to see but not easy to prove in a laboratory. This type of manifesting happens because we respond to the power of the universe and allow ourselves to stay open to what it has to tell us and what it wants to do with us. When this happens we find we can create the best life we are capable of living. That is when the "deep driving desire" to live the fullest version of ourselves steps into our lives.

This third type of manifesting is what this book is about.

Introduction

First, I set an intention.

— Oprah

J. K. Rowling said it best when she said, "We do not need magic to change the world, we carry all the power we need inside ourselves already."[1]

This book is about exactly that—it is about the power that you have at the deepest level, the Soul level, with which you can manifest all that you are capable of creating.

It's possible to manifest from other levels, of course, but much of what we manifest when we are not connected with the Soul is created from a place of fear rather than from a place of love. These manifestations tend to be negative.

To understand this process of positive manifesting we'll need to look at some very impressive people, so we can see how in each case they have allowed their Soul energy to lead them to manifesting at their highest personal level. We'll be able to learn from their hard-won lessons and see that we're not very different from them.

I think we've all noticed the great celebrity figures of our time and most of us have probably asked ourselves, could my life ever be like that? These are the people who seem to move effortlessly through their lives. Doors that seem shut to everyone else fly open at their touch. Perhaps they make us look inwards and ask—why isn't my life working like that?

So what is it that those high-profile people are doing that the rest of us aren't? Is it just luck, or that they're better looking, or better connected , knowing the "right" people? How did they get to be where they are? Is it a question of their "deep driving desire"? And what does that mean, anyway?

We know the answers to these questions, and we're going to share them with you. What you'll find is that the secret of their success is something that's readily available to each and every one of us. Once you understand how this works you, too, can set about transforming your life.

So, first and foremost in this book you'll find a practical guide to how you can mobilize this transformative power, which we call manifesting. Knowing about it and putting it into action will allow you to achieve the highest possible version of yourself.

Secondly, this is the story of three powerful women who have all manifested significant things in their lives. By following their life stories we can learn exactly how manifesting works. We can find out what we must do, and what manifesting can do for us.

The three women we'll be looking at are all well-known figures—Oprah, J. K. Rowling, and Anita Moorjani. They are from the United States, from England, and from Hong Kong, which shows us that geography and cultural background has no stranglehold on how manifestation works. It can work anywhere, and with anyone, if you know how to use it. What you'll see is that for each of them, manifesting brought them far more than they could ever have predicted.

This could only happen because they are, each of them, in alignment with their authentic being, and this allows them to fulfill the intentions of their deepest selves. We could call that their ability to listen to their Souls.

It's not a complicated process, but it does require us to pay close attention to what's actually going on.

Let's take a look at these three extraordinary women. They've achieved the highest version of themselves in very different fields, so it might seem odd to link them together. But if we look beneath the surface we'll see some powerful similarities. For example, it's remarkable that each one rose from a place of despair and difficulty, in some cases from terrible poverty, to become the leaders and role models they are today. Their situations were so hopeless—and yet they became supremely successful in their fields. From a normal, logical, linear perspective their success could never have happened—everything was working against them, or so it seemed. That's why we think they're such good examples of manifesting.

Take a look at Oprah first. She started life as poor, abused, and suffering under racial prejudice. Her best friend Gayle King describes her situation: "To say that she was very poor would be very kind."[2]

That didn't hold her back. She became a talk-show guru and as we know now owns her own studio, Harpo Studios in Chicago, and the OWN network. But it was never about the fame, for her. She has often said she sees herself as primarily an educator working within the Oprah Winfrey Network. Becoming a teacher so she could make a difference in the world, she says, "was the burning in my heart."[3] That was always her intention, one that was not attached to a specific outcome. It came from listening to her Soul. She didn't want to be famous because she wanted adulation. She wanted to be well known so she could use her position to help others more fully. As she said in Oprah Magazine, "Teaching is my true calling . . . It's what I'm called to do."[4]

J. K. Rowling's story is very similar in many ways. She also rose from poverty to worldwide fame, but in an entirely different way—through writing the Harry Potter novels. She rarely appears on television and seldom makes public appearances. She is in some ways the complete opposite of Oprah. Yet she too has reached millions, with over 450 million copies of the Harry Potter books sold. Her overriding desire, she has often said, is to write, to communicate what she feels. She has always been more interested in the truths in her stories than in the monetary rewards. Her aim is to teach, also, using the stories as a way for children and adults to think about what they can contribute to our world. And she has often said that the most powerful thing in the world is love. She truly knows the power that love has. She was the world's first self-made billionaire writer—and she only lost that status when she decided to give a huge portion of her wealth to charity.

The third woman we'll be looking at is Anita Moorjani. She came to public attention for a completely different reason. She was in the final stages of lymphoma, in a coma, when she spontaneously healed and astonished all her doctors and relatives by her total recovery from a cancer that was expected to kill her within hours. Now she lectures, touring the world, speaking about this experience that opened her up to understanding the core value by which she lives, and that is love. She sees this as her way of giving back to the world in gratitude for the life she now has.

You could hardly choose three more different people, working in more different ways. Yet they all have something in common. They all managed to turn their lives from potential disaster to astounding, miraculous success in a way that cannot be explained by normal logic. If they started in a situation of potential disaster then you can certainly turn your life around, too—if you use the principles described in this book.

Wouldn't you like to know how they did it?

Part of the answer to this question is that each of them faced, with courage, the horrors of finding themselves at rock bottom in their lives. Discovering the strength that lies on the other side of life's struggles made all the difference.

Let's look at this a little more closely and see how the experience worked for each of these women.

Oprah has spoken frequently about being poor, black, and female in a deeply racist corner of a profoundly racist Mississippi in the 1950s and 1960s. She was raped at nine and pregnant at 14. These are traumas that could have destroyed anyone. Yet through it all she knew she had more to do in the world than to settle back into a life of poverty, degradation, and hopelessness. She was not going to be anyone's washerwoman or housemaid. She wanted to help others empower themselves, since she knew first-hand what it felt like to be disempowered.

This is her chosen way of bringing a profoundly loving force to the world.

To understand part of the difficulty of Oprah's journey we can look at what Wayne Dyer once said about her:

Many years ago Oprah Winfrey was interviewed about her life and asked whether she had known that she would become one of the most powerful women in the world. She explained to the reporter that when she was a little girl, someone asked her what she wanted to do with her life.

She answered by saying that she didn't know. She just liked talking to people. The person quickly retorted, "Well, you can't make a living doing that." [5]

So many people told her she couldn't get anywhere by doing what felt right. They wanted her to stop being her authentic self. And how wrong they were! She succeeded by doing what she felt was absolutely true to who she is, and by following that feeling with passionate devotion.

J. K. Rowling also faced potential disaster. She found herself practically penniless with an infant to support and no husband. She describes herself as being "about as poor as you can get without actually being homeless."[6] And yet, despite everyone's advice to the contrary, she kept on writing her stories. She didn't remain in some safe, dreary job as almost everyone she knew encouraged her to. Even when the first Harry Potter book was about to be published, her editor urged her to take a teaching job since she was very unlikely, he said, to be able to make a living as a writer.[7] She ignored that advice. Even though she'd been a teacher earlier in her life, she had no intention of returning to it as a career. She kept on doing what she felt was true to the core of who she was despite the difficulties. As she said, "It was my life and it was very hard; I didn't know it was going to have a fairy-tale conclusion."[8] In her commencement address to the graduating class at Harvard in 2008 she said, explicitly, that no one should ever underestimate the value of experiencing failure. And she is quite certain that the core value conveyed by her books is that love is the most powerful thing of all.

Just like Oprah, she decided to live her truth, no matter what anyone said. She elected to do what she felt was true to who she is, and do it with devotion.

Anita Moorjani's experience was even more dramatic. She was at death's door. Relatives had gathered at her hospital bed for what were expected to be her final hours. And in those last few moments, when she was already in a coma, when her internal organs were shutting down, she suddenly realized that there was something more she was supposed to do on earth. Drifting closer to death, she experienced the wondrous sensation of being wrapped in total love, before finally agreeing to return to her body. Her body then healed itself, as if by a miracle.

Anita describes this event as her coming to a realization of who she actually was at her core; and her core was love. The cancer that had grown and taken over every part of her body now left her completely within days, banished by the power of her new-found connection with love. We could say that living her truth is what saved her life—and her Soul.

These three women all share this essential attribute of choosing authentic living. More than this, though, is that they chose to stay fully engaged with that authentic life.

Each of these women could have chosen to give up at any point. But they didn't. Instead they chose to connect to what was authentic in themselves, and in the process they connected to the source of all energy in the universe, the power of Love. They express that love in very different ways. But all these ways are authentic to the core of who they know themselves to be.

What we need to notice here is that there are many more than just three ways to connect to the source of energy the universe provides for us every day. There are as many ways as there are people. We each have our own way, our own task that we must do, and it is up to us to live in faith and to find it. For when we do what we truly feel, and when we do it with courage, then we can access our full power to manifest what we need, effortlessly. The universe supports the authentic self.

In some ways we could say that each of these women was in a space in which there were no other options open to them but to align with the power of the universe. There simply was no place left for them to go, and nothing left to lose. Even so, it takes courage to keep on doing what you feel you must do.

Many other people have been in that space of feeling at rock bottom, also. Some of them stay there. And that is because for a variety of reasons they do not connect to themselves and so they cannot reach the source of the universe's power. Perhaps their despair is so deep they simply cannot hear what the source is telling them.

The point to remember is this: We always have a choice about how we react to a difficult situation, and some people do not act positively. Others find themselves freed by the experience. That is exactly what J. K. Rowling says of her situation, when she was at "rock bottom."

*I really became myself here [in her small apartment in Scotland]
in that everything was stripped down. I'd made such a mess of
things. But that was freeing. So I thought, I want to write. I'll
write a book. What's the worst that can happen? It gets turned
down by a publisher. Big deal.*[9]

She found in herself the freedom to do the one thing she truly cared
about—write. It's very close to the way Anita Moorjani describes her
experience of being at the lowest possible point in her life—on the
brink of death. At that moment, hovering between worlds, she knew
she could either give up or decide to take up the challenge of living
an authentic life. Here is how she expresses it:

*Even though I always had a choice, I also discerned that there
was something more . . . [she then continues, using italics to stress
that this was what she thought at the time]. It feels as though I
have a purpose of some sort yet to fulfill. But what is it? How do
I go about finding it?*[10]

We need to focus on this important point for a moment. Anita knew
there was something still to do in her life that her Soul was asking her
if she wanted to complete. She didn't know exactly what it was she
had to do, but she decided to accept the challenge. She stayed open
to possibilities and listened to her Soul.

Oprah puts it this way—she says that her experiences allowed
her to feel fully her spiritual self, and that she chose to honor that
above all. She knew that she was "a spiritual being having a human
experience."[11] It's a phrase she's repeated often, and it's an important

one if we're to understand her success. She simply didn't see herself as a human being trapped in the rules and laws of the human world. That human world would have subjected her to a limited life if she'd allowed herself to accept its view of who she could be. She chose to connect with her sense of her essential spiritual self instead. And when we connect with spirit we connect with the power that created the universe. That is when we become manifesters at the highest level.

J. K. Rowling has spoken eloquently about her experience of being in deep poverty and depression. In her Harvard graduation address her main theme was how failure had brought her close to despair, but what she discovered was that "rock bottom became a solid foundation." She goes on to explain: "Failure meant a stripping away of the inessential. I stopped pretending to myself that I was anything other than what I was . . . I was set free."[12]

Sometimes abject despair—in J. K. Rowling's case she suffered a clinical depression—can lead us, eventually, to where we need to be. Rowling had every reason to be depressed; her marriage had failed, she was in total poverty, and she had a baby to support. Anita Moorjani was actually dying, but that moment of almost losing everything freed her mind so that she could see why she had become ill in the first place—because of the fear of not fitting in. Each of these women stopped trying to fit in, and that allowed them to change everything. Instead of listening to the voices outside, those insistent voices that demanded conformity, they listened to their own inner voice. They listened to their inner voice; they listened to their Souls.

Listening to your inner voice is not something most of us do easily or naturally. The world tends to ask us to look outside ourselves rather than inside. What we can say about these three women is that hardship made them able to listen to their inner being and so to rediscover their Souls. What they discovered was that their Souls had plans for them, things they wanted them to do. This is what we will call the Intention of the Soul. To understand this fully we need to look closely at the word "intention."

Oprah has frequently said *The Seat of the Soul* by Gary Zukav is her favorite book other than the *Bible*. In this book Gary Zukav defines intention this way: he says it is "the quality of energy that infuses your actions."[13] In other words it is not what we do, it's what we are feeling when we take the action. For example: anyone can give money to a cause; but some people, as we know, give money only in order to be seen as generous. Perhaps they want to look good. That intention is not pure or selfless and it will certainly affect the outcome of that deed and the giver's life. Looking good for a moment will not solve the giver's problem, which is that he probably spends most of his life not feeling good enough. In contrast to this, if we give money or support out of compassion and love we are much more in tune with the loving part of our authentic being. The intention is pure because it is not looking for any reward. This pure intention comes from the Soul.

At such times we are most fully the best version of ourselves—love allows us to hear what our Souls have to tell us. It is the Soul that connects us to the creative power of the universe because it is, and always has been, at one with that energy. In conversation with Oprah, spiritual teacher Panache Desai said that when we are working from this place of purity we are honoring our "Soul signature."[14] Oprah agrees. Our intentions need to come from our authentic self, from the connection to the Soul, or they cannot be as fully powerful as they need to be. A selfish intent is no intent at all.

This is what we mean when we say living from the place of love is a way to contact the Soul. This is the powerful force that causes manifestation, which we saw described as a "deep driving desire" at the start of this chapter.

If we know this we can now see how the entire process works. When we use the word Source what we mean is the primary creative energy of the universe, the same power that created the planets, the stars, microbes, plants, jewels, and each of us. This endless creativity is what we are part of—except that many of us don't know that yet. The Source has created our Souls, every single one of them. Each Soul is always in contact with the Source and yet every Soul exists on earth in order to grow and learn certain lessons.

Only when we are aligned with our Soul do we allow the flow of energy from the Source to move through us so we can manifest the very finest aspects of our destiny.

So we can say that every Soul arrives on earth with certain lessons it has to learn, that it wishes to learn, and that it therefore has an agenda, an intention. This series of lessons is specific for each and every one of us, and only by listening to the inner voice of our Soul can we find out what it is we are here to learn.

The three women we're looking at are evidence of this, and if you listen to happy and fulfilled people anywhere in the world you will sometimes hear them say things like, "I was born to do this" or, "Whoever would have guessed I'd wind up doing this? But I love doing it." These are the people who have listened to their inner voice and have found out what their Souls need them to do.

Throughout this book we'll be asking you to focus on your spiritual self, and showing you in practical ways how you can do that. Along the way we'll be referring back to these three powerful women—Oprah, J. K. Rowling, and Anita Moorjani—so you can see how they handled their life challenges. Those challenges were as big as anything any of us face. You, as you read this book, may say, "Oh, I've never faced that kind of problem" or "I've never had a near-death experience," but that is not the point. The challenges these three women faced were extreme, yet we all face obstacles that are a little like theirs every day. Some of us have more challenges, some of us have fewer. Anything that threatens to move you away from living in alignment with your Soul is a serious threat. It could be worrying about how to pay the bills, or fear about a sick child, or concern about how to take care of one's aging parents. If it takes you away from living life in your spirit then it is a serious threat to your ability to manifest at the highest level.

Our Intentions with This Book

Since this is a book about intention, one of the first questions we have to deal with before we go any further is, what is our intention, as authors, in writing this book? And does that intention come from our Souls?

There's no trickery here. Our intention is to guide you, the readers, towards the recognition of something that is very undervalued—the intentions that come from the Soul. As you read these pages and see how events have unfolded for others, you'll understand how this process works so that you can use it to become the best possible version of yourself.

We'd like you to be aware of this information for a simple reason. We think the world needs more people in it who are operating at their highest levels, working towards loving, peaceful goals. We also know that doing this is what we all need for a fulfilled, abundant, and beautiful life. We'd like you to have that life.

It all comes down to this: When your intent is in accord with the universe, things start happening. That's when manifesting happens at the highest level.

That's quite a claim, so we'd better point out that the key word here is intention, and that there are at least two different sorts of intention. The first is when we decide we want to do something specific. So, for example, an intention can be very direct, such as: "I intend to go to the gym more often!" That's a good intention, but we have to ask where it is coming from. We may say this from an intention to get fit or perhaps so we can impress our friends. It's an intention, right enough. But it's an intention that serves the intender directly, and which seeks a specific result. It is at its core exactly the same urge as the desire to look good by giving money we have just looked at. Because of this we can say it comes from the rational part of the self. It's really a calculation, not an intention. It's designed to get you what you want—a better body, a longer life, a more attractive physique, or any number of other definite results.

There's nothing wrong with that sort of intention. We need those intentions in order to do many things in life. It's just not what we'll be focusing on here.

The intention we wish to guide you towards is different, because it comes through you, rather than from you. It comes from your Soul and your feelings, not your thinking. Imagine a situation where a mother goes to the gym not because she wants to look good but because she wants to make sure she stays healthy so she can raise her children properly. That's a different kind of intention. Often this sort of loving intention takes the form of an intuitive urge that tells us to do something. That something, whatever it is, will bring us closer to real fulfillment in life. It is your Soul seeking to guide you. An intention like that does not fade.

The difficulty we experience is that this kind of urge may seem illogical—and so we tend to distrust it if we don't know what it is. People around us may tell us to be suspicious of such feelings. They'll tell us to dismiss them and be sensible. Don't follow that desire to volunteer at the homeless shelter, they may say, when you could use the time to earn more money elsewhere. Or perhaps they urge us not to do what we love but to take the safe job that pays well. And yet, as we'll see from these pages, often that is exactly the wrong response. Here's how Gary Zukav describes the way intention works: "Feel the intentions of your Soul. Feel not what your mind tells you, but what the energy of your Soul tells you."[15]

The pure intentions of your Soul will rise into your awareness in exactly this way. You will recognize them because of the pure energy of love and clarity. That's how you know they exist. You can ignore them or entertain them. If you ignore them nothing much will change in your life and your Soul will remain exactly as it is.

When the intention is pure—when it is not self-serving—it leads us to miracles. Some of those miracles will astonish you just as they astonished Oprah, J. K. Rowling, and Anita Moorjani. They didn't know what the future would be. They just followed their inner voice so they could feel their Soul's intentions, and so manifested a larger life than they'd ever imagined. The future is woven with your intentions. Following these pure intentions will bring you to where you need to be. If you'd like to know how to listen for a pure intention so that your life can be fulfilling and extraordinary, read on.

Now, before we go any further it's important to realize that listening to your Soul may not make you as wealthy and famous as these three women. That's because wealth and adulation are simply the froth on the cappuccino. They are by-products that can occur if you decide to live an authentic life. Everyone's circumstances are different. You may not become immensely wealthy following the intentions of your Soul, but you will find the universe will support you. You will get what you need and you will certainly discover something far more valuable—the deeper wealth of living a fulfilling life that has significance to you and others. That's a different kind of wealth.

Although these three women are very different, they certainly understand the path that each of them is on. Oprah is completely open about her admiration for Rowling's Harry Potter novels; she sees them as spiritual stories. Talking with Panache Desai about the scar on Harry's forehead, which Panache described as a reminder that Harry always has his "Soul signature," she agreed enthusiastically. "I remember the first time I read and saw that. I wished I had that." Oprah said, "But what that is, is the part of you that knows you already do [have it]."[16]

Like Harry, we are all blessed with a powerful identity that comes from the Soul. The scar on his forehead will not let him forget who he is at the deepest level. And, just like with Harry, the world will try to divert us so we forget that inner Soul identity.

When we choose to live from the connection we have to the Soul, from a pure intent, we must listen to its whisper. And then anything is possible—although it may take some effort along the way.

The Six Steps

To show how this works we're going to take you through six distinct steps, giving practical guidance about how to deal with each. Here is an overview for quick reference.

First: You'll have to recognize that you are a Soul.

People will try to tell you that you are all kinds of things—a son, a daughter, a taxpayer, an employee. These definitions will tie you to the material world and they won't help you because you are, first and foremost, a SOUL. You are a spiritual being in an earthly body.

Second: You'll need to create alignment with your Soul.

Once you know you are a Soul inhabiting a body, you have to find ways to let the Soul part of you become the most important part of who you are. This means you'll have to work from what you feel to be fundamentally true for you, rather than from what seems like a reasonable plan for dealing with the world. That means you have to pay attention to the energy of your Source. This is the task of identifying your "Soul signature" and responding to it. Put it this way: some people stay in jobs they describe as "Soul-destroying" for the sake of the paycheck. Even though one cannot literally destroy one's Soul, staying in this kind of situation creates painful experiences of powerlessness. Those experiences really will destroy the connection to the Soul. If you choose to respect and honor your Soul, you simply cannot live like that anymore. That's a frightening thought for some people, since we all love security and a job very often is a form of security, as well as being an identity. But once you know you are a Soul you can choose to start making the changes you need to make.

Third: You'll need to stay in alignment with your Soul.

Living every day from the Soul is not always easy, and certainly many well-intentioned people will tell you to be "practical" and "realistic." That often translates into not living in alignment with your Soul. This is real pressure, and it's hard to shrug off. At this point you'll need to take very good care to stay in full alignment with your Soul, and you'll need to listen very carefully to what your Soul tells you. You'll know when you're aligned with your Soul because that is when you will feel most fully and unapologetically yourself. Note, this is a feeling, rather than anything specific that one can point to.

Fourth: You'll need to identify the intentions of your Soul.

If you've reached the third stage you'll discover that your Soul has plans for you. It has things for you to do, some of which you are not fully aware of yet. It will keep nudging you towards possibilities that you might not have considered before and which may seem illogical. You'll need to take the time to listen to those hints and then act on them, without second-guessing yourself. This takes courage and practice because it might not make sense from a rational and logical perspective. That's because everyone's Soul speaks its own language, a language that only you can understand. You know when you have an intuition, or a hunch. When you see something and suddenly know what you need to do. No one else can tell you.

Fifth: Your job is to manifest the intentions of your Soul.

This is an important point. If you've moved through the first four steps you'll begin to realize, to feel, that your Soul is connected to the energy of the universe, and what you'll discover is that the universe offers you opportunities to do certain things that will grow your Soul. It may be calling you to be an artist or a teacher or a parent or anything at all—and your job is to recognize the call that you feel in your Soul. Whatever the call is, you can be certain you do not know where it will ultimately lead, but it will lead you where you need to be so you can be the fullest version of yourself possible. The energy of the universe will lead you forwards—if you cooperate with it. This is what Oprah, J. K. Rowling, and Anita Moorjani felt. This is also what countless people we have encountered have told us: when the universe gives you hints, if you follow them, you will move gradually towards where you need to be, using all your abilities for the good of yourself and of others.

Sixth: When you work from the intentions of your Soul the universe will support you, and you will manifest what you need.

The universe wants you to be healthy, joyful, loving, and to live a fulfilling life. It can only make that happen if you follow the intentions your Soul will communicate to you. It does not fail. Your Soul is always connected with the boundless energy of the universe, and this is where manifestation happens effortlessly. The universe is creating everything around us ceaselessly, in vast and generous profusion, so we can use this energy consciously and wisely.

These are the six steps. We'll be shaping the book around them, so you'll be seeing them again in each chapter.

IN A NUTSHELL

1. Three impressively influential women of our time—Oprah, J. K. Rowling, and Anita Moorjani—have something in common; each one decided to follow her own inner prompting.

2. This inner prompting comes from the Soul's intentions.

3. Listening for this inner voice requires us to be true to ourselves, rather than to what others expect us to be.

4. Looking at the experiences of these three women, we can see six steps that will help us to respond to our own Soul's intentions. These are:

   ① Recognize that you are a Soul, not just a body.

   ② Align yourself with your Soul, not with the outside world's demands.

   ③ Stay aligned no matter what anyone says, and listen to your Soul.

   ④ Identify the intentions of your Soul.

   ⑤ Know that your job is to manifest the intentions of your Soul.

   ⑥ Know that the universe will support you and proceed in confidence.

PART ONE

Recognizing That You Are a Soul

Chapter 1
The Evidence: Stories of People
Undergoing a Soul Experience

◆———————◆◇◆———————◆

For truly we are all angels temporarily hiding as humans.
— *Brian L. Weiss*

Perhaps you find it hard to believe that we are Souls as well as bodies. Many people doubt it. Yet there is plenty of evidence that suggests that we are, all of us, far more than just the bodies we inhabit. We're going to review some of this evidence now.

What Anita Moorjani experienced may seem completely unbelievable, yet the staff of the hospital to which she was admitted with stage 4b terminal lymphoma (cancer of the lymphatic system) have the detailed medical records that show the actuality of her transformative near-death experience. Anita has spoken about this event freely, and her book *Dying to Be Me* describes it eloquently. As you'll see, this title is absolutely appropriate.

What happened to her sounds like something out of a movie. She was rushed to hospital in Hong Kong, where she lives, in what doctors believed was the final stage of her cancer, her body swelling badly, and she was deep in a coma. Her organs were beginning to shut down, and the doctors informed her family that this was the end, they could do no more for her.

What they didn't know was that Anita's sense of this event was completely different. As it was happening she saw herself from above, from outside her body. She could hear every word the doctors and her relatives said, and she realized that she had spent her whole life living from a place of fear, afraid of what others would think. "I gave my power to the world outside, and external events had the ability to control me—my behavior, moods, and thinking," she writes.[17]

When she felt this she knew, somehow, that she hadn't finished whatever it was she needed to do on earth because she'd been too busy trying to be "normal." Suddenly, she felt flooded with unconditional love. With great reluctance she pulled herself away from the peaceful haven offered by death, and willed herself back into her body. The message, the thoughts she heard in her mind as she lay in the coma, have resounded in her mind ever since: "Go back and live your life fearlessly."[18]

What happened next astonished everyone. The tumors that had been so prominent on her body, all along her spine, began to shrink— by 70 percent or more in a couple of days. Her internal organs began to function again. She came out of her coma and, much to everyone's surprise, she knew all about the medical discussions her doctors had agonized over—even when those discussions hadn't been in the same room.

Within days she was sitting up, talking, eating without a feeding tube for the first time in weeks. Her cancer was completely gone.

The doctors couldn't believe what they were seeing. Neither could anyone else. In fact the medical team spent several weeks testing her to see where the cancer had gone, and they were deeply puzzled to find absolutely no trace of it.

Anita is now a persuasive, powerful speaker and communicator and what she has to tell us is important.

What can we learn from this? First of all, her experience lets us know that we are more than just our bodies. Looking down on her own body in its hospital bed, she knew this.

Second, her ordeal lets us know that we have a purpose in life, all of us, and it involves living with courage. Not living this purpose, by comparison, will kill us.

It took a while for Anita's purpose to become plain to her. Her near-death experience could, she realized, help others see their illnesses in a new way. She says, "I suddenly realized that both my getting cancer and healing were actually for the planet . . . to serve as an instrument of healing to take place in others."[19]

In fact her message has already gone far beyond her own experience, and people all over the world who have heard of her healing have started thinking differently, not just about healing, but about their relationship to Source, and what that means for them. Her mission is about healing in the very highest sense of the word. She is helping to heal us all, by bringing us back to our Souls. Her "Soul signature" became plain to her—and now she is living it.

The third thing we need to pay attention to is that she knew her Soul was linked to something much larger, something we could call Source or a world Soul, which contains all wisdom, all love, and all healing. The title of her book, *Dying to Be Me*, really does say it all, because she had to face the disturbing fact that her old way of living was killing her, and that as she faced death she was given the opportunity to be fully herself in its highest form. She chose life, and to embrace love, and so she became who she truly was all along capable of being. She realized she was a loving Soul, and not just a body.

We are all like Anita. We are Souls first, and bodies are the clothing we have so we can operate in our world.

You may feel that Anita's experience is too unusual to be credited. If so, you can do no better than to look at what happened to Dr. Eben Alexander, whose 2012 book, *Proof of Heaven: A Neurosurgeon's Journey into the Afterlife*, declares itself fully in its title. Dr. Alexander is a distinguished specialist in his field. He taught at Harvard Medical School and in a career that spanned 25 years he worked at Brigham and Women's Hospital and at Boston Children's Hospital. In fall 2008, he spent seven days in a coma suffering from meningitis. He was not expected to live. Towards the end of that time his doctors viewed his brain scans and declared that he was definitely brain dead; he would not recover. They could detect no brain activity.

Yet he did recover and is now fully healed. Looking at his brain scans, now, he can interpret them from his viewpoint as a trained neurosurgeon and know that he was by any measure dead. No one doubts this. But he is alive today, and he knows that during that time when he was technically dead he saw many things, most significantly a "brilliant orb of light" that he knew to be God.

Bear in mind that this was a man who had stopped believing in God or religion many years before this event. He believed only in science. His experiences have startled many people because he is a plain-speaking man of science who, suddenly, was surprised by an experience of his Soul.[20] His conclusions are worth looking at closely, since he now says that: "the brain . . . dumbs down a higher consciousness."[21] It is this higher consciousness that connected him back to the power he calls God, although he freely admits that this concept of God is much bigger than he can find words for. The normal actions of the brain—the everyday thoughts and concerns and worries we all tend to have—were what stopped him from knowing his Soul existed.

Dr. Alexander's experience is every bit as dramatic as Anita's, and equally well documented by hard scientific data. Each had an experience that had nothing to do with "normal" life and everything to do with the Soul. And just like Anita, Dr. Alexander has now made it his life's work to alert us all, especially the medical establishment of which he is such a respected member, to the existence of the Soul and the limitless love that awaits us on the far side of everyday consciousness. Dr. Alexander and Anita have come to know each other, and they totally agree that we are Souls attached to bodies.

This leads us to some important considerations. Primarily, we have to recognize from this that we are more than just our bodies.

If we think about our bodies we have to admit that they are always changing. As babies we had one sort of body. As teenagers we had another sort of body, and at twenty we probably felt that we were our bodies and nothing more. Yet, as we grow older, that same body changes. All the cells in it completely renew themselves every seven years, such that no single cell is still alive after that time since they've all been replaced. Bodies seem to be closer to a sequence of temporary houses that we get to inhabit for a while. When we see that, we have to admit that we are more than our bodies. We can call that "consciousness" if we wish. Anita Moorjani would say that it is the consciousness of being a Soul.

Knowing that your Soul exists is a game-changer. We can't ever think the same way about ourselves again. And here's the point: near-death experiences (NDEs) are fairly plentiful. Look around and you'll see just how plentiful. For example, in 2012 singer George Michael went public about his NDE, which he'd had when in a Vienna hospital, and he talked about how he wrote one of his songs especially about it. That song is called "White Light"—because that is part of what he experienced as he hovered close to death.[22] You may have read about this and other similar events. There's even a highly respected research foundation that examines such phenomena.[23]

In an NDE very often the person who is undergoing the trauma is likely to report seeing bright white light, feeling wrapped in limitless love and acceptance, and then returning to the body they left, knowing that there is some task they need to do before taking their eternal rest. These are the dramatic examples. But in fact we all have this experience available to us in a more familiar form. Many people you talk to will be able to pull up an occasion when they were nearly killed, and yet survived. If you are one of these people are you going to shrug it off as luck, or are you going to ask: "What is it I'm supposed to do with the rest of this life that has been so miraculously spared?" If you've had some experiences of meaning and depth beyond the five senses, are you going to ignore them? This is exactly what happened to Dr. Eben Alexander. He could have kept quiet, but he chose to risk the judgment and rejection of his medical peers rather than not tell his truth. He stopped worrying about his reputation as a man of science. Anita took the same risks. People could have ignored her as a crazy person. She chose to speak her truth instead. Both of these people discovered that they had something important to tell the world.

Oprah describes something similar, although in a rather different way. She has spoken frequently about her sense of her needing to do more, to be more, so that even in the darkest times of her life she knew she was fired with a purpose she had to pursue. This is not mere ambition, nor is it the desire to make money. It is a sense of recognition. She knows she has been given the bountiful gift of her abilities, which she now feels expected to use widely. She knows she could so easily have faded into anonymity if she hadn't held on to her inner sense of knowing. That's what the Soul is. That's what the Soul does.

J. K. Rowling experienced this a different way. She relates how she was on a long railway journey and the train was delayed for several hours, and how, in the midst of this, the notion for the Harry Potter series came to her.[24] She could have chosen to read a newspaper instead, but she decided to explore the ideas and develop what the story needed to be, all the time knowing that this would be a series of books, not just a single volume. As an unpublished author she would have had every right to reject this fantastic idea out of hand. It would take too long to write! She had no inside contacts to get her published! Give up now!

But she didn't. She knew something important had come to her.

For each of these people the universe turned out to have far bigger plans for them than they could ever have had for themselves. The good news is that, when you make full contact with your Soul, it seems that others who have also discovered their own Souls tend to gravitate towards you, and the effects are multiplied, sometimes in unexpected ways. Like-minded Souls tend to help each other.

The Soul is at work even when we don't call it that. For example, Steve Jobs, the late CEO of Apple, didn't use the word Soul much. What he said at various times, and most memorably at the Stanford University commencement address he gave in 2006, was that we should do what we love: no excuses. When we're doing what we love we are doing the thing that feels absolutely authentic to us at the deepest level, and that is at the level of the Soul.

And here we must draw a distinction: compulsive activities and addictions are not something we love. Most addicts would admit that they hate their addictions and themselves most of the time, except they feel they can't face the world without their chosen drug. That is not the same thing as doing what you love and loving what you do. Jobs described how he felt compelled to explore the inventions and innovations he created—it wasn't about the money. It was about doing what he had to do. That is the Soul at work.

This is exactly what J. K. Rowling says, also, in a slightly different way. She puts it very simply: "I write because I love it."[25] It's an activity that engages her completely and she knows she has a profound belief at the core of her writing. That belief is that "love is the strongest power there is."[26] It's what she shows throughout the Harry Potter series, which is surely about those young wizards discovering that they are far more than just bodies who can do unusual things. They know they are Souls and they know they have a task to do.

We are Souls, but we are also human beings living in a material world. Sometimes this means that we strive to fit in and live the conventional life, the safe life. We get scared about the future and not having enough to survive, and so we agree to do what everyone else in the material world is doing—which is to focus on facts like money. There is part of us that likes this. And so our Souls are sometimes overwhelmed by that part of the self, which is created by fear. But at a certain point we can't keep living like that. Perhaps we have a near-death experience, or a severe shock that wakes us up from our ego-dream world. When that happens we see that we are Souls, that we always have been, and that the best way to pay attention to the Soul is to listen to and cherish our inner voice. Anita Moorjani describes beautifully how she felt so much love for those she knew and that she was herself wrapped in universal love, as she hovered between life and death. She realized that, rather than being powerless and insignificant, she was a powerful Soul. In an interview Anita said: "I learned that when we are at that centered place everything that is ours will come to us."[27] When you are aligned with your Soul, miracles happen and you don't have to create them from a sense of effort. They just happen because you are in harmony with the universe. That is manifesting.

This is what is at the center of finding alignment with your Soul. If you are aligned with your Soul you simply can't be aligned with the fearful parts of your personality. What does this mean? Well, sometimes we become so involved in trying to impress others that we forget who we actually are. And this comes from fear. This is the part of us that wants things or influence in order to feel good. Think of this as the frightened part of the personality from now on. This frightened part of the personality simply doesn't want the same things as the Soul. The frightened aspect of me wants to focus on what I have and what I don't have, and how that makes me look in the eyes of my friends and neighbors, and it'll keep me worrying and obsessing about that for my whole life if I do not challenge it.

This is the part of the personality that craves reassurance from owning things, from having everyone's good opinion, and from having status. As we know, these are all things that come from outside us and, if we live in the good opinion of others, then we will surely die if that good opinion fails—as it inevitably will. This is the part of each of us that is a bit like a pop star who always has to be in the limelight. When the public attention fades, real distress is the result. This frightened part of the self can derail anyone. The only answer is to try to heal it. And we do this by recognizing that real self-valuing comes only from within ourselves.

IN A NUTSHELL

1. Take a moment now to review the evidence we've presented here that we are Souls. It probably seems fine on paper, but I expect you're hanging back and thinking—"It worked for them but it can't work for me." That's very natural. That's your mind trying to stay rational and protect you. The trouble is that your protective rational mind has got you to precisely where you are now. We'd like you to be able to move higher. We'd like you to think about a bigger life for yourself.

2. Moving into this new Soul space will take courage. People will tell you you're mistaken, and some of those people will be your friends and family. They'll try to talk you out of it "for your own good," and because they love you. Sometimes they'll do it because they don't want you to succeed. You're going to need real courage to move into contact with your Soul in the way we're suggesting. So don't tell everyone what you're doing, at least to begin with. Hold this notion close, like a newborn child, and protect it from the storm.

3. We all have frightened parts of ourselves—the parts that worry about what others think of us. We all want to be liked and accepted. Yet feelings like this can also stop us from spiritual growth because we tend to do what others expect of us, rather than what feels true to our Souls. If we give in to this fear it will stop us from manifesting anything.

Chapter 2

Why We Should Be Interested in the Voice of the Soul: Finding the Authentic You

+———————◇———————+

If I create from the heart, nearly everything works; if from the head, almost nothing.

— *Marc Chagall*

The first objective is to find what the authentic you, the real you, actually feels like.

The real you is the most healthy, grounded part of your personality that is aligned with your Soul. How does it feel to be connected with this? It feels optimistic, loving, open, and it does not feel judgmental or ready to condemn others. Above all else you will feel a deep sense of joy, even in the midst of difficulties, because you'll know that difficulties are just a small part of life, not the whole of it. Some people have described this feeling as being a bit like being in love—that moment when you realize that, even though there will be struggles ahead, you want to face them anyway because you know you'll be with the person you love.

Unless you have met and welcomed this part of yourself, this Higher Awareness as we might call it, you cannot begin to manifest.

That is because without this first step you cannot hear the voice of your Soul.

Some people call this awareness the Higher Self. Others call it the Higher Intelligence. Both these terms seem to suggest being better than other people, and that's a notion we cannot allow. You will not be better than anyone, or worse than anyone—but you will be more awake than you were before, because you'll be more aware of a larger and more harmonious version of who you can become—the authentic you. That's why we'll be using the term Higher Awareness.

Finding the authentic you is simpler than it sounds. You just have to stop doing what you think you ought to, and start being who you are.

How does this work? Eckhart Tolle has an exercise he takes people through in which he has them simply focus on their breathing. You could try it now. Sit quietly and focus only on your breathing, and how it feels. Other thoughts will arrive, but see if you can just let them go. Spend a couple of minutes doing this. When you're done, you may find a few things to ponder about this exercise. For example, when we become aware that this miraculous thing, the body, is regulating itself without our conscious input, we notice a strange thing; we have thoughts that have nothing to do with the body. We don't need to think about how to breathe, digest, circulate our blood, and so on. Our body takes care of that for us. Meanwhile, our thoughts can go anywhere we choose. We can decide to think about lunch or about our creative projects or next week's staff meeting. We get to choose. So we must ask, who is the "I" that is doing the choosing? Sometimes we feel we aren't choosing at all, because our thoughts circle ceaselessly around some troublesome aspect of existence that we'd rather not think about. So the recognition we come to is this:

If I would rather not think these thoughts then there's a separation between me and my thoughts. I am not my thoughts, therefore. I must be more than these thoughts.

A good way to think of these kinds of thoughts is as mind-chatter. They take up a lot of our time but they're not who we are.

This ability to observe who we are, and observe our thoughts, is the first step in noticing that we have a Higher Awareness, a part of us that can observe what we're doing, and then choose well or badly. We can be annoyed with a friend, a co-worker, or a child and still we can behave kindly. This part of us can choose to act with love or with fear. It is not reactive, and it does not lash out. The Higher Awareness, when it is healed and whole, always chooses to act with love and this is what connects us to the Soul. Your Soul is much bigger than you are, since it is connected to the Source, the energy of the universe. This means that the thing we normally think of as "myself" on earth is only a small part of who each of us is. We're going to call that smaller aspect of us the personality, since it's made up of who we are physically and psychologically, and it develops depending on how we interact with our environment—our family, our community, our culture, and even our country.

Sometimes we can gain a powerful sense of our personality as being only a part of ourselves when we look at photos or videos of ourselves. These days, when every phone has a video app, we can do that easily. Take a look at a brief video of yourself. Most of us will not be thrilled with this idea, and will immediately start to notice flaws in our appearance. If you can suspend that critical aspect of yourself for a moment, you can ask—who is this person, truly? Our personality cares about whether we look good; but our authentic self cares more about whether this is a true representation of who we are inwardly. And just as film stars and TV celebrities use video to check the way they present themselves and refine their image, so we, too, can notice that the way we habitually "are" is something that has been built up over time. At such moments we become aware that we have an authentic self—which may not always be on display.

This is very much like what happened to Anita Moorjani when she felt herself outside her own body. It wasn't until she moved out of her usual sense of self that she was able to see herself objectively, and realize that there was more to her than she had wanted to admit. She saw that she had a body and a personality, and that the "more" that existed was her awareness of herself as a Soul.

For her and for us the personality is the way we choose to interact with the world. It changes over time. Like our skin, it is part of us, but it's only a small part of the whole experience that is each of us. We can decide to live by what our skin and our sensations tell us, or we can pay attention to what our inner awareness tells us about the whole of our experience—the Higher Awareness.

When we listen to our Higher Awareness we tune in to the voice of the authentic self, which is where we hear the voice of the Soul. As Oprah experienced in the beginning days of *The Oprah Winfrey Show*: What she discovered was that just being authentically herself—compassionate, kind, real—caused extraordinary things to happen.

The show became a phenomenon. It truly was. [. . .] The lesson that this taught me over the years is —anybody pretending to be anything other than who you really are, you will never ever reach your personal potential. You cannot do it. [28]

Oprah describes beautifully how she simply set aside the trappings of mere personality, of hair and looks and whatever TV expected her to be. When she did that she could be genuinely present to her audience. Being fully present is always a gift, an act of love, one that meant she was operating from her Higher Awareness—and that this is a way for her of being in touch with her Soul. That is the root of her success.

If you are genuinely present to others, and with yourself, if you listen with your Soul it always allows you to connect fully to your Higher Awareness. The Higher Awareness is the authentic you, and being in that space allows you to be in touch with your Soul. Your Soul is always connected to the Source.

It sounds simple, so why can't we get in touch with our Souls right away? It's a good question, and, as we've already seen, there are different parts within each and every one of us that get in the way. To some extent the frightened parts of the personality are in a constant struggle with the Soul to get the upper hand. The frightened parts of the personality are those parts of us that are not authentic. Who we really are is the Soul, and we can gain full awareness of this through listening to the Higher Awareness. The Soul is the true, authentic you.

Accessing our Higher Awareness is not a one-shot deal. It is a process. As we learn to trust our intuition more, as we learn to let go of the noise generated by the wounded and frightened parts of the personality, our awareness will grow. We will see that we are more than just the information that comes to us from the five senses, and that we have the ability to feel ourselves as multisensory. The multi-sensory person finds others to be loveable because he or she sees the loving core within the other, no matter who they choose to be. The Hindi greeting *Namaste* can help us here. Freely translated, it means,

"The divine core of me greets the divine core of you." At such times we look past the surface imperfections and into the Souls of others. When we do this we move beyond the idea of "me" and "others" because we see we're all linked. Divisions like that are illusory, and serve only to make us feel separate from others. Of course, we still have to live in the world, work, and pay taxes. The ego we already have is good at that. But the Higher Awareness is something we have access to that exists at the same time. It allows us, for example, to see that we have been wronged (a wounded ego reaction) and yet it allows us to forgive (a Higher Awareness choice).

It takes some practice to live like this, if only because it's so easy to slip back into our old self-protective suspicions about others. These are the frightened aspects of our personality that tell us we don't matter unless we look good, or unless we're obviously successful in worldly terms. Most of us have felt this kind of fear. It leads us to see our own value only as it is reflected in the eyes of others. It's very much like junior high school. As such, it will stop us doing what we feel we need to do, and it will persuade us to do what we think everyone else will be impressed by. When this happens we are cut off from our Higher Awareness. The more we can use our Higher Awareness the more powerful it will become, and the closer we will be aligned with our Soul.

If you truly want to access your full manifestation power and want to have the full support of the universe you will have to learn to align with your Soul. As long as you are creating from your frightened parts, you will not be creating from your true highest potential and you will not be creating from who you really are and what you really want. You can create a great deal from the fear-based parts of the personality—but it will not satisfy your spirit. It will merely flatter your vanity for a while. These fear-based parts of the personality need constant reassurance—more toys, more drama, more events and vacations.

Once we've become fully aware of the Soul the second task is to find what its Intentions are.

It may very well happen that your frightened ego wants something other than what your Soul wants for you. When that happens you cannot work from your full power and potential. If your frightened aspect wants you to be a lawyer because the money is good, while your loving aspect wants you to be an artist (where the money can be precarious), you will feel conflicted. Perhaps you will take the "safe" option. Many people do. But if you do you will be going against your Soul and your actions will not be empowered.

So if you really want to have access to your full creative manifestation power you will first have to understand what your Soul wants, and not your frightened ego.

Listening to your Soul is not difficult. All you have to do is allow it some quiet space and it will speak to you. What it says may surprise you, because it will sometimes seem crazy or illogical, at least at first. Your task is not to dismiss it out of hand. Accept its suggestions as hints; think about them. Inspiration is not always dramatic. Sometimes it's just a feeling that this is the right thing for you to do, now. When you act on these notions unexpected possibilities open up for you. This is when you will start to notice manifesting is working for you.

The Soul will speak to you in ways that are very specific to you. If you are a visual person perhaps it will speak to you when you look at pictures, or paint them. If you are a person who likes words your Soul may lead you to recall what you have read, and it may lead you where you need to go as you write, when new ideas appear before you. If you are musical you may hear something that inspires you, or you may compose a song that goes deeper than you expected. Many people have reported hearing wisdom spoken by children they've been caring for. Our task is to be open at such times. Then we have to act on what we feel.

As you start to act and create from your Soul, you will find that your life begins to fill with meaning and vitality and purpose. This is because you are moving in the direction that your Soul wants you to go. If you follow the voice of the Soul then you will have the full support of the universe and you will find that you are part of a series of events that lead you to live the life you were born to live.

Some people think that "the full support of the universe" means that everything will be delivered to them on a silver tray. Do not make this mistake. The universe will give us many opportunities to grow spiritually. At times it appears to throw boulders in our way. Why would it do that?

There's an answer to this. It does this so we can learn from the temptations and grow stronger spiritually. The universe offers us many chances to be the strongest people we can be. Remember, Jesus was tempted in the desert; the Israelites were tempted when they worshipped the Golden Calf; even the Buddha was tempted. Only a robust and thoroughly tested Soul will be able to achieve its full strength, and therefore its full ability to manifest. We don't know what we can do until we're challenged, and that's when we exceed our expectations. That's when we grow. The Soul wants us to grow spiritually, and so it leads us to a spiritual gym to help us grow spiritual muscle.

For Oprah a huge opportunity to grow spiritually came when she found her TV ratings were under threat and she was tempted to move towards sensation-based entertainment. As she relates it, one day she was interviewing neo-Nazi skinheads and she began to realize that by giving them airtime to vent their hateful ideas she was not improving the world she knew. Her response was deeply authentic and totally moral. She took some time to be alone and it came to her that she had a duty. What she heard was: "Take the higher road."[29] She has held firm to this ever since. Ratings and sensational TV were never her central concern again. "It was more important to me to be a teacher," she says. This was not a temporary feeling or one that could be easily disregarded. She has never stopped using her programs as a way to raise public awareness about important issues, and she has gone on to found her own school for girls in South Africa. She has worked tirelessly for these beliefs, even through difficult times. She's shown us that following your Soul's prompting is the best way to honor your own truth.

J. K. Rowling has also had her temptations, one of which stands out especially for her. Michael Jackson, then the King of Pop, wanted to do the musical version of Harry Potter. Rowling refused. And even though the idea may seem bizarre to most of us, how many people could have turned down the money and the Hollywood glitz? Only someone who truly believed in the value of her work could have done that. Rowling has also turned down multiple highly lucrative offers to have her characters used in various advertising initiatives. These came from industry giants like Sony, Microsoft, and Boeing, so they were not small temptations.[30] McDonald's even wanted to sell Harry Potter Happy Meals—but she turned them all down.[31] It's never been just about the money for her.

Indeed, her sense of personal integrity has surprised some of her fans. After she completed the Harry Potter series she was under considerable pressure from the public and her publishers to keep on writing and produce sequels. She decided not to. Her novel *The Casual Vacancy* is an adult novel full of adult themes, but it is, she says, what she felt authentically called to write. With her 2013 mystery novel *The Cuckoo's Calling* she even went so far as to write it using a pseudonym. She could have assured herself of huge sales if she'd used her own name. She chose not to, because writing, for her, has never been about feeding her ego.

Anita Moorjani talks about this in a slightly different way, but the situation is roughly the same since even now she often feels the pressure to be someone she is not:

> *I don't have to try to live up to other people's expectations of perfection and then feel inadequate when I fail miserably. I'm at my most powerful when I allow myself to be who life intended me to be.*[32]

The point is clear. When we listen to our inner guidance we don't have to worry about anything.

The important thing to realize about such temptations is that they are not sent to derail us. They are opportunities that allow us to grow spiritually. When we are tempted we can entertain the notion of doing something; we can explore it, and begin to imagine what it feels like to follow that desire. In the process we bring to the light of our awareness the dark and less than admirable parts of ourselves. Every time we do this we challenge the frightened parts of the personality and we have the opportunity to grow spiritually. Once the frightened parts of the personality are exposed, out in the light, we can see them as they really are. Usually they're to do with fear.

An example will help here. Perhaps we desire to take a short cut, to do something slightly dishonest. Usually we are tempted to do this because we're not sure we're worthy of getting things honestly. Imagine a person who is not honest on his resumé so he can snag a better-paying job. The result is that although he gets the job he lives in terror of being discovered. So the fearful part of the personality, the part that prefers lies and wants to get ahead using lies, manifests only more lies and more fear. That is manifestation in action. You don't manifest what you want, you manifest what you are. If you choose to be dishonest you will manifest more dishonesty. In contrast, in the case of a temptation we get to imagine this scenario ahead of time. We experience it and above all we feel it as a real possibility. Is this really what we want? Do we truly want to live with the feeling of dishonesty that will follow? Why would we want to do that to ourselves? Why would we be so unloving?

When we see things this way we can choose very differently.

Awareness like this is not theoretical. It's a genuine confrontation. And when we see what it involves we can choose what is right. It also allows us to see that part of who we are, wanted to choose what was wrong for us. That is the part of us that needs healing. Temptations are always useful because they bring to our awareness those parts of ourselves that need healing. So, instead of working from fear and deception, we can decide to operate from courage and love to heal that fearful part of who we are. Most of us have these areas in which we're weak, areas that drain our energy. Temptations are one way we can bring them to light, face them, and heal them by taking actions that allow us to live differently, in the place of love.

IN A NUTSHELL

1. The voice of your Soul is important if you want to manifest at the very highest level. You will first have to find the intentions of your Soul, otherwise you will tend to manifest only at the level you are at now—which means you won't manifest to your highest potential.

2. The intention of your Soul is so important because your Soul is linked directly to the vast creative power that is the universe. As such it has access to far more possibilities than you could ever imagine. You will never reach your highest potential if you do not connect with your Soul.

3. It won't be easy all the way, because the universe will give you tests—which are opportunities to grow spiritually. It does this to build your strength, your focus, your inner courage, and to help you to become truly whole. When these opportunities come, try to be grateful, for they are always there to heal you. Recognize them for what they are and know that you will only be given opportunities that you can learn and grow from. They are there to teach you vital truths and allow

your Soul to reveal its full potential to you. The opportunities are not like a test in school where you have to study hard
beforehand and there is only one right answer. An opportunity operates more like an expedition that allows you to see
how much more you have to offer that you weren't aware
of yet. Anita says it perfectly when she writes: "I already am
all that I could attempt to be."[33] Our job is to become fully
aware of that. We are not meant to be perfect, we are meant
to be whole.

PART TWO

Finding Alignment with Your Soul

Chapter 3
We Have Access to a Higher Awareness

◆ ·◇· ◆

I've come to believe that each of us has a personal calling that's as
unique as a fingerprint—and that the best way to succeed is to discover
what you love and then find a way to offer it to others in the form of
service, working hard, and also allowing the energy of the universe to
lead you.

— Oprah

If we are to align with our Souls we'll need to develop our capacity
for Higher Awareness. Let's take a look at this Higher Awareness and
how can we have access to it.

In order to align with your Soul you need first of all to access your
Higher Awareness. Accessing your Higher Awareness doesn't mean
you have to be super-smart. In fact, some super-smart people are at a
real disadvantage. They're the ones who can always find a reason for
everything but can't enjoy anything. Intelligent people can be like
that sometimes and fail to contact their Higher Awareness.

Let's think of this a different way. Your body, the flesh and blood
and bones that make up your physical being, can be compared to a
laptop computer. It can do a lot of things, this computer. But now,
try thinking about this Higher Awareness as the electricity that

powers the computer. With it that computer can do anything. Without it the computer will soon exhaust its batteries and become just a large object a bit like a kitchen cutting board. We can only gain access to its full power by connecting a cord from the wall socket to the power input. And that's a pretty good description of how most people are with their Higher Awareness. Most of us have the computer but we've lost the cord. We know we have a Higher Awareness, but we've forgotten how to access it.

How could we lose such a vital piece of equipment?

It can happen a number of ways, but this is what most commonly happens: As we grew up we were taught by our parents and in school to use our logical thinking above everything else. Logical thinking means linear thinking and reasoning. It is all based on cause and effect and also on the perception that we are five-sensory beings.

This means that we were raised to trust only what we could perceive through the five senses—what we can see, hear, smell, taste, and touch. However, in thinking like that we really are not giving ourselves enough credit because we are more than five-sensory beings. We already have access to a much higher source of intelligence—we've just been taught not to trust it. And so we try to ignore anything that doesn't fit our five-sensory world picture. We've all heard the statement, "I'll believe it when I see it!" But what if that isn't the whole picture? After all, it cuts out a lot of possibilities. J. K. Rowling addresses this in a way that is highly comical when she has Harry's uncle and aunt, the Dursleys, refuse to believe in Harry's magical powers. They don't want to admit what they see, even though he obviously has them. Panicked by what they don't understand, they pretend it isn't real.

As we've seen, Anita Moorjani's whole life is about exactly this. She was constantly attempting to live the life other people wanted for her, and so effectively she shut out her Higher Awareness. She disconnected herself from her Soul. It nearly killed her.

And yet we know that we have a Higher Awareness because we have imagination. Imagination is what creates things. It allows us to think that we could be more than we are. Everything you can see around you was, at one time, just a flicker in someone's imagination. Because of our imaginations we've created space shuttles and rockets that go to Mars and the computer micro-processor that allows me to write these words right now. Everything came from that Higher Awareness that dared to ask—what if there were more possibilities? We can call this ability *intuition*.

The truth is that we have a bigger sensory system than we think, one that can give us information that our hands and ears and eyes and nose and taste cannot usually give us. That creative power of the imagination is part of the ceaseless creativity of our universe, which is always making new growth and new possibilities available to us. We can connect to that powerful source of energy. That is what the Soul does. It uses our loving parts to connect us with the Source. And its chosen method of doing that is through intuition, which always speaks directly to our Higher Awareness.

In practical terms this means that we suddenly have more options. We don't have to see things the way we've always seen them. For example, the person who is rude to you is not necessarily singling you out. Perhaps that person is in a place of suffering, and so is in a bad mood. Our Higher Awareness allows us to see the situation differently. We can choose to see it with compassion and love. We can choose to see beyond the poor behavior of the personality that is presenting itself to us—and that allows us to respond from the Soul, where our Soul sees the other person's Soul.

This is at the core of what our Higher Awareness is, because it asks us to see beyond the surface and consider the human and the spiritual values that lie beneath the obvious.

When we do this, when we allow ourselves to think like this, a remarkable thing happens. We notice that things are much better than we thought. We start to live from a place of love rather than hate. We seek harmony where before we may have been in competition with others. We find we can cooperate rather than being fiercely independent. We find we are generous where before we had been withholding. This all becomes possible when we act from the Soul.

When we truly live from this space, with our whole being, this Soul space draws more love and compassion and cooperation to us. We manifest more of what we live. This is at the center of manifesting from the intentions of your Soul. So, let's look at some examples of the way the Higher Awareness works.

It works first of all through intuition. Most of us have been in a situation where we've had a sense that it's time to pay attention to a gut feeling we might have. Perhaps we've got a deadline, and our rational mind says, "Don't pay attention to anything else—just carry on!" It seems sensible. But what if at the same time our Inner Self tells us we would be better off taking a break? Very often this is our Higher Awareness, our deep intuition, telling us that something simply doesn't feel right, and we should wait until it does. Perhaps some vital piece of information that will change everything will pop up at the last moment. Perhaps we'll discover that this Higher Awareness is alerting us to real danger ahead. Or perhaps that irrational sense that comes to us to stop driving, now, is because our Higher Awareness knows that some danger lurks just ahead of us—even if our rational mind has yet to know this. No doubt we can all recall times when we had an overwhelming intuition that we didn't respond to. That's the feeling of "if only . . ." that seemed so impossible to believe at the time, but which turned out to be so accurate. Most of us have experienced this.

Or here's another example: possibly we've been holding off making a phone call because we think our friend ought to call us this time. Yet it just might be that the urge to call that person needs to be obeyed because the individual is in despair and too depressed to reach out to others. If you ask people, you'll be astonished at how often each of these examples have actually happened. Yet each is inexplicable in "rational" terms.

Our Higher Awareness knows things that we could not possibly know rationally, and it's surprisingly accurate. Wallace Stevens, the great poet, described it this way: "Perhaps the truth depends upon a walk around the lake ('Peter Quince at the Clavier,' 1915)."[34] Often we have to step back and listen to the inner voice that can tell us what is true. But we can't hear that voice if we don't give it any space.

Perhaps you've had an experience like this. Sometimes we speak more wisely than we know, or someone we were not expecting to have any real insight delivers a statement that takes our breath away. At such times the Higher Awareness is breaking through, almost despite what we think we're doing. The therapist who speaks exactly the right words at the right moment, and so allows for a change that might not otherwise have been possible—such a person is also working from a

Higher Awareness. We might also consider the many TV programs currently in fashion in the US, like *The Nanny*. The main character in the program intuitively knows how to communicate with the unruly and difficult children concerned, win their trust, and change their behaviors. And the result is almost magical, in every case. Those people do not have doctoral degrees in psychology—they just observe the situation, assess it, and then they act in love. That's the Higher Awareness at work.

Our Higher Awareness works for us every day, if we listen to it, in another slightly different way. It always guides us towards joy. This is because joy is the way we respond when we know we're doing something that feels authentic and valuable. It's not always the laugh-out-loud kind of joy (although it can be). Mostly it's a sense of calm happiness and directedness. Anita echoes this when she says, "I now live my life from joy instead of fear."[35] This is exactly in tune with J. K. Rowling's statement that she continues writing, "because I love it." In the same interview she declared, "Should I be more diplomatic? Oh, I don't care. No, there is literally nothing on the business side that I wouldn't sacrifice in a heartbeat to have an extra couple of hours' writing. Nothing."[36]

Here's how it works.

Imagine you hate your job. Perhaps you don't have to imagine that! Your rational mind says you have to stay in the job for the money. Your Higher Awareness begs you to stop torturing yourself and leave, because by staying you are being unloving to yourself and to others. This is because the Higher Awareness recognizes that we manifest our lives best when we are in a state of happiness, and it wants us to get back to that place.

So you decide to leave that ghastly job. All your friends tell you you're crazy, but you feel free to breathe for the first time in months. Now, it may not be the case that you immediately get a better job. The situation may turn around immediately, or it may take a while. You may have to be patient. But the change can't happen while you are stuck in the old, rational mindset.

In fact, sometimes we do have to be very patient indeed. What's this, we ask? I thought the Higher Awareness would lead me to the right place! Where's my new job?

This is where some people give up. What they don't understand is that the universe is always offering us opportunities to grow spiritually, just as we've already described. In this case it's a situation that brings to light the tendency to give up. This temptation exists because it offers us the chance to recognize it, reject it, and so become the best and strongest versions of ourselves we can be. It offers us the chance to trust the manifestation process by being patient. If we don't trust this process totally our actions will not be empowered. And so things may be a little uncomfortable for a while. Perhaps it turns out that we don't need a new job, but a new way of looking at the life we have. And so we wait, and we discover we can easily deal with the waiting. It's only the frightened part of the personality that has problems with waiting. The more you begin to see that every experience is an opportunity to choose between fear and love, the more you start to trust the universe. And each time we choose love we're manifesting from the Soul.

The process is really pretty simple. Let's sum it up.

IN A NUTSHELL

1. To access our Higher Awareness we have to LISTEN to what it says.

2. When we hear it, we then have to TAKE ACTION based on what we hear, even if others oppose us.

3. Then, after we take action, we have to TRUST that all will go ahead as it is meant to. We have to let go of the expectation that the result will be exactly what we thought it would be. Why? Because it will be better than we thought. When we do what we love we are already leading fulfilled lives, and that fulfillment is part of the reward. You won't be preoccupied with any future outcomes because you'll be happy with what is happening right now. Did Oprah think she'd be one of the richest and most influential women in the world? No. She did what she loved to do. Did J. K. Rowling believe that Harry Potter would be a worldwide phenomenon? No. She thought she was having a great time writing the books and that one day she'd get published. Did Anita Moorjani imagine she'd become an inspirational speaker and writer? Not at all. She simply wanted to tell her story. What appeared was much bigger than their imaginations could frame at the time.

4. What they did was they followed their Higher Awareness and took their risks, boldly. That's when they manifested new lives.

Chapter 4
Aligning with Your Soul, Aligning with Source

✦ ───── ✦◇✦ ───── ✦

You are joy, looking for a way to express. It's not just that your purpose is joy, it is that you are joy. You are love and joy and freedom and clarity expressing. Energy, frolicking and eager, that's who you are. And so, if you're always reaching for alignment with that, you're always on your path and your path will take you into all kinds of places. We will not deny that you will not discover miracles, and create benefits and be involved in creation, and that you will not uplift humanity—we will not say that you will not find satisfaction in so many things you create, but we can't get away from the acknowledgement that you are Pure Positive Energy that translates into the human emotion of joy.

— Abraham-Hicks

Now that we know more about the Higher Awareness we can use it to move closer to understanding manifesting.

Once we recognize that we are Souls, and that our Higher Awareness brings us into contact with that Soul, we can listen to what it has to say. As we do that, as we listen, we create our connection to the Source. Now we need to make sure we are fully in alignment with the Source. The Source, as we will recall, is the endless creative power of the universe. It's the power that is ceaselessly creating and destroying stars, planets, and every cell in your body.

How can we understand our connection to Source? Think of it this way: imagine apples on a tree. They're all individual items, and we can buy them by the pound. This makes us think these apples are separate. Notice, though, that each apple is connected to a branch, and each branch is connected to the trunk, and the trunk is connected to the roots, which are laced in complex patterns and run through the soil, and the soil is part of the land that miraculously provides all the growing energy for whole orchards of apples and fruits and crops. The apples could not appear without the rest of the tree and the earth in which it grows. Each apple is slightly different, too, and each apple tree produces slightly different sorts of fruit. And here's the point: we are the same as those apples. We may think we're different and special, but actually we're all connected. And just like apples we carry the future generations in us, generations that will flourish, miraculously, whether we live happy lives or not. We are just the most recent crop of the divine creativity of the world.

We are like the apples; our Higher Awareness is like the branches and our Soul is like the tree; but Source is the endless creativity of the universe that created the world and the earth the tree grows in. Source, in its endless generosity, is a form of love bigger than anything we can easily understand. But our Souls recognize it.

When we see that we are expressions of the creative power that runs through everything, just like those apples, we have to rethink who we are. We have to see that our true identity, the deepest part of who we are, is not about how we look or our possessions. Here is Anita Moorjani again:

I discovered that we're all spiritual, regardless of what we do or believe. We can't be anything else, because that's who we are— spiritual beings. We just don't always realize it, that's all.[37]

Once we see this we have to learn how to align with this new sense of self. This is the Law of Manifestation: you align yourself with your Soul and find its intention, and the organization of the universe, the Source, begins to show up in the most magical ways for you.

The intention to manifest anything has to come from what the Soul needs and not the frightened parts of the personality. In other words, it's not about what you want in terms of shiny toys and so on. This is important. Most people can't manage to see this. In fact, every day people are manifesting things, but because they are not fully connected with Source all they can manifest is more of the same condition they are currently in, right now. So the anxious person manifests more things to be anxious about; the poor person manifests more poverty; the unhappy person manifests more misery.

To manifest fulfillment, abundance, and love we must listen to what the Soul tells us, using our Higher Awareness to connect with the power of the Source. That power is the limitless creativity of the universe, a loving universe that created us and everything we perceive. In these pages we'll be showing you how you can do that work most effectively.

The Laws of Manifestation are actually very simple. What they say is that when we pay attention to the inner voice we align with our Souls. When we are in tune with our Soul we can manifest its intention, and so we move into harmony with the creative power of the universe, the Source, because our Souls are part of this Source, and always have been.

When we are in alignment with it we are making full contact with the power that created everything.

So let's spell this out:

Our task is to align ourselves with our Source, and find its intention. You are capable of attracting all the things that your Source is capable of attracting.

To do this we'll have to notice that we are Souls, first and foremost.

That requires us to see who we actually are, rather than who we think we ought to be according to someone else's value system. That's the task of our Higher Awareness. It keeps us true to our authentic self.

So you have to change your current self-perception and see the reality of yourself as a powerful Soul. Now, that statement will cause many of you, as you read this, to pull back. You may feel this is a thoroughly arrogant assertion for anyone to make. You're probably thinking something like this: "Me? A Powerful Soul? What right have I to say that? What would my pastor/rabbi/priest/ayatollah say to that? I'd be in trouble if I said that!" This kind of thinking will keep you in a small and obedient world.

The truth is that every religion you can name acknowledges that human beings were created by a loving Creative force, one that's eager to have those human beings achieve spiritual enlightenment, a full connection with the Divine Source. The implication is plain. We are capable of becoming the great Souls that the creative power of the universe wants us to be, because we are part of that power. We can receive this loving power by opening ourselves to our Souls. We only imagine that we are not part of this marvelous creation. Anita Moorjani calls this our "magnificence,"[38] and she sees it as who we truly are when we're fully connected.

IN A NUTSHELL

1. We are Souls. Souls are not something we have, or own, they are the center of who we are. But the Soul is also bigger than who we are. As we walk around our world we exist as temporary expressions of our Souls, incarnated into human bodies. Sometimes we believe we're only those bodies. We have to remember that we're actually expressions of our Souls.

2. If we bring ourselves into alignment with the Source and its intention by listening to our Higher Awareness, we can manifest anything and everything that the Source wants. It is not our intention but the Source's intention that matters.

3. And this is an important point—we cannot manifest anything new and better until we recognize that we are Souls and become fully connected to the Source. Unless we do that all we can manifest is what we have already manifested, the situation we currently are in.

4. If we wish to change that we'll literally have to "up our game" and see ourselves as spiritual beings who need to live in a spiritual fashion, in a place of acceptance, love, generosity, gratitude, and reverence for life. This is the loving space the Soul needs us to occupy. This tends to go over poorly with our neighbors, who want us to be like them—materialists, realists, and "practical." We're urging you to stop being purely materialist.

5. If you want to manifest at your very highest level you must align with this universal creative power and find its intentions. Source can see much further than you can. It can do things you may never have dreamed of. And it can take you to places that will surprise and delight you. Best of all, it will take each and every one of us outside the box of our own familiar mindsets. Here is Anita again: "If I restrict myself to only what I'm able to conceive, I'm holding back my potential and what I allow into my life."[39] Or as Oprah puts it, "God has a bigger dream" for each of us.[40] J. K. Rowling, shaking her head in disbelief at the way her life has unfolded, said, "it never occurred to me in a million years"[41] that her life would be as phenomenally successful as it has become.

6. Is this what you want? The choice is yours. You always have a choice. But you wouldn't be reading this book if you didn't want this.

Chapter 5
Why It Is Important to Listen to Your Soul

+——————— ⋅◇⋅ ———————+

The world is confusing; your spirit is not. The opinions of others are
confusing; the wisdom of your inner voice is not.
— **Sonia Choquette**

Why does this matter so much? Couldn't we just listen to good advice
and be satisfied with that? It's a good question, and it leads us to
some important clarifications about manifesting.

The thing we'd like you to notice is that manifesting happens all
the time, for all of us. It never ceases. Since this is the case then we'd
have to say that the world around us is manifesting a fair amount of
strife and unhappiness. And that would be true, because not everyone
is manifesting from the best part of themselves. It seems pretty clear
that some people are manifesting from the frightened parts of the ego.

In direct contrast to this, if we choose to listen to our Higher
Awareness we can tune in to our Souls, and so we will manifest at
the highest level of which we are capable. We'll be operating from
the very best part of ourselves. If we do not know about this, we'll
do whatever we see around us and we'll tend to manifest only at
our ordinary level of awareness. In that case we'll get exactly what

we already see around us all the time. This is what we could call "collecting"—we simply amass more of the same things and experiences that we always have done in the past. Nothing much can change at this level. Fortunately, when we are at this ordinary level of awareness things tend to arise that are challenging, as if the universe is asking us to think differently. Sometimes that means we get a wake-up call and start to listen to our inner voice. That's good! But if we allow ourselves to become discouraged by these events we may find that we discard our awareness and slip down to a lower level; and at that point we tend to manifest things that are not at all good for us. In this situation we may even believe that we're helpless victims. This is where the miserable person begins to see the world as unhelpful and alien, and so manifests more alienating and miserable experiences. All are genuine manifestations; yet it's easy to see which ones might serve us best.

If we remember to stay in contact with the Higher Awareness we will always be operating from the Soul, out of a space of love and compassion. Since we manifest what we are, rather than what we want, by living in this way we will inevitably manifest more occasions on which we can experience loving and compassionate events, even if we are not sure what the ultimate outcome might look like. So for example, we could think of the man who wanted to manifest a van so he could take food to homeless shelters. This loving impulse did not result in a brand-new van appearing in his driveway overnight. Instead he listened to his inner voice, discovering that this was exactly what he felt was needed. Then he declared his intention, talked to people, and very soon a friend of a friend who owned a restaurant and a van agreed to turn up each evening to do the job and provide more food into the bargain. At the end of the day our manifester didn't own the van; he didn't have to. What he got was the use of the vehicle, an added source of food for the homeless, and the lasting friendship of the van owner, who was only too delighted to be able to be of compassionate service to others. And so the love grew.

Just imagine if this man had chosen to operate out of a slightly lower awareness. He might have set his mind on owning the vehicle, in which case he'd have had to raise money, or perhaps take out loans. The whole process would have been very different, although it could have worked.

Now, imagine the effect of all this on the manifester. If he'd not spoken about his desire, if he'd kept quiet and given in to despair when the van didn't appear magically, he might have doubted he'd ever get a vehicle at all. He would simply have manifested more despair. This would be an example of how he would have manifested at a level far below his normal level.

This example is important because plenty of people have good and loving intentions and yet they give up when they feel the universe is not responding in the way they expect. The universe is always responding. If we want its best response, though, we have to make sure we're putting our best awareness forwards, and we have to expect that things may well go in a different direction than the one we planned.

When opportunities arise, and they will constantly arise before us, we will have to choose which ones are worthy of our attention. We have to make sure we're not slipping back into the frightened ego space of wanting to look good. Our task is to do whatever will create more good in the world, more love. Your Higher Awareness is supremely good at knowing this. That is what your Soul wants.

IN A NUTSHELL

1. We can choose the level at which we wish to live, and when we do so we will manifest from that level of awareness.

2. If we do not listen to the Soul and respond to its messages then we will manifest only at the level at which we are currently living, or perhaps even at a lower level.

3. If we want to be the best version of ourselves we must use our Higher Awareness, stay open to possibilities, and listen for the voice of the Soul, so we can manifest fully.

4. The key element is love. We must always ask what the most loving way forward might be, and then aim for that.

Chapter 6
How Can We Connect with the Soul and Define Our Destiny?

◆——◇——◆

To me education is a leading out of what is already there
in the pupil's Soul.

—*Muriel Spark,* **The Prime of Miss Jean Brodie**

If you wish to connect with your Soul using your Higher Awareness you'll need to recognize the importance of stillness and gratitude. Gratitude is always a way to establish a Soul connection. You'll need to seek out inner quietness so you can listen; and you'll also need to acknowledge a feeling of gratitude so that you can receive the messages you'll hear in the stillness. Then your Soul will speak.

In her column "What I Know for Sure" in the Oprah magazine, Oprah talks about defining destiny and the importance of listening to the voice of the Soul.[42]

What she points out is that as early as 1992 she deliberately decided to change *The Oprah Winfrey Show*, moving it from being sensational and confrontational TV aimed at getting ratings to being a show that took what she described as a "higher road." Her major focus from then on would be to establish real connections between people and encourage personal growth. Her aim was quite simple, and broadly educational—she wanted to help people think differently about themselves. Particularly she wanted to encourage them to explore ideas about the Soul and what a more meaningful life might look like. Clearly, this was not business-as-usual TV programming.

This decision was not about money or ratings. It came from a loving desire to use television to raise personal consciousness rather than just to provide entertainment. It turned out to be an enormously popular alteration. People were hungry for the sort of programs Oprah offered—in defiance of the accepted ideas about what kind of television was supposed to appeal to viewers. It proved so successful that in due time it led to the creation of the Oprah magazine, Oprah Radio, and the Oprah Winfrey Network.

Here's what Oprah says about this:

Using my voice as a force for good: It's what I was meant to do. And I got here by listening to the still, small voice that I felt so strongly one evening on my grandmother's back porch when I was a girl.[43]

Oprah was raised as a Christian and she describes this awareness in specifically Christian terms, but we can see without too much difficulty that she is describing the connection to her Soul and the power of the universe. She was responding from her authentic self, and not to whatever the media gurus were saying.

All my life I have looked to God for guidance. In the early 90s I started to recognize that I wouldn't survive if I continued to play

the TV game my competitors were playing. One day while vaca-
tioning in Colorado, I went into the woods to quiet the noise of
the world and contemplate my next move. I remember standing
among the golden aspens and asking the voice that has been a
comfort for so long: "What would you have me do?"

The answer came as it had when I was a girl: "Take the high
road."[44]

Oprah is absolutely convinced that she was responding to heaven-sent advice. The way she describes it we could call it the voice of God speaking to her. Whether you believe in a Christian God or some other type of divinity matters less than that we notice what she was doing. It was her willingness to listen for what the divine energy of the universe had to say to her that matters, not the exact words used to describe that entity.

In the terms we're using here it was this inner voice, the voice of her Soul, that was directing her. And it did not give her bad advice. This is what she says about it:

The decision to listen to this voice—against the advice of many
of the stations that carried my show—is the reason I still have a
show. If I had ignored it, I would have disappeared into the void
of defunct broadcasting. There's a long, long list of talk shows
that have come and gone since I started.

What I know for sure: Often we don't even realize who we're
meant to be because we're so busy trying to live out someone
else's ideas. But other people and their opinions hold no power in
defining our destiny.

What has made me successful is the ability to surrender my plans, dreams, and goals to a power that's greater than other people, greater than myself.

Before making any major moves, I first ask: "What would you have me do? Who would you have me be?"[45]

Learning to connect with the Soul in this way is paramount for any lasting success. Oprah has made it a major part of her life and her decision-making. It is really more of a feeling than a voice, she says. Oprah calls it "a whispery sensation that pulsates just beneath the surface of your being."[46]

J. K. Rowling describes it slightly differently, but in terms that are equally compelling. Speaking of her novel *The Casual Vacancy*, she describes how the idea came to her while on a plane:

And I just knew. I had that totally physical response you get to an idea that you know will work. It's a rush of adrenalin; it's chemical. I had it with Harry Potter and I had it with this. So that's how I know.[47]

Knowing something in this way is, for Rowling, a physical feeling, experienced not with the head but with her whole being. Your Soul may speak to you in any number of ways, but its hallmark is that sense of inner knowing that cannot be denied. That is what it feels like when your Soul responds to the call.

One of the main points we can take away from this is that if you go against your Higher Awareness and the voice of the Soul you will inevitably find yourself at odds with the natural flow of the universe.

You may do a number of things well, but it will always feel like it is a struggle against yourself. It may, in fact, make you feel physically unwell. In bygone centuries the word for this was "Soul-sick."

The most important aspect of listening to your Soul is that it will tell you what your own individual and authentic path will be. This path will feel right, even if it sometimes feels hard. And here you have to remember you cannot follow anyone else's path.

Many people have seen Oprah on her show, or read a J. K. Rowling book, or listened to Anita Moorjani speak, and they've said—I bet I could do that. I'm sure many have tried. But if you do that it won't be authentic to who you are. So here's some advice: Don't try to be Oprah. Only Oprah can be Oprah. She lives and breathes what she does every second of her life, and she loves what she does. All three of these women love what they do. It's up to you to find out what your passion is, what really motivates you, and then stick with it. The universe asks you to be fully yourself, not a pale imitation of someone else. Only Elvis could be Elvis.

You may find that the authentic you is somewhat less dramatic than your frightened ego would like it to be. But it's not about showing off, it's about being fully authentic.

How can we learn to listen to and connect with the Soul?

This question is at the very core of aligning our personality with the Soul. If we can create this alignment we will, as best-selling author Gary Zukav tells us, be creating Authentic Power.[48] Authentic Power comes as a result of learning to distinguish the voice of the Soul from the chatter of your mind. It means choosing the voice of the Soul no matter what's happening inside or outside of you. As Ralph Waldo Emerson said, the aim is to be still, to turn within.

The first requirement for this process is stillness. Let's look at this more closely. Unless you create a space of stillness within yourself you will be divorced from your Soul, and this is your chief guiding force when setting intentions. There are many ways to connect with the Soul.

One way to connect is through being in nature. Oprah went into the woods of Colorado to quiet the noise of the world and contemplate her next move. Anita urges the same thing, although for her the sea is a powerful force that centers her. Rowling has spoken frequently about her love of the Forest of Dean in England, because she feels she can be truly alone in a forest, with her own thoughts. The character of Harry Potter echoes this since the feeling he gets from the beautiful grounds of Hogwarts is roughly the same—he learns to center himself when in natural settings. When you are at one with nature you can become a whole being with a Soul and brain and spirit all connected to your Source.

In this space you will become aware that the answers are not somewhere out there in the world; the wisdom is within you.

It's not always so straightforward, though. If we recall Harry Potter's situation at one point in *Harry Potter and the Deathly Hallows*, he is camping in the woods wearing around his neck a horcrux in the form of a pendant. Even though he is in a natural setting he finds that this horcrux has the ability to pollute his mind with thoughts of his inner worthlessness. When Ron takes the pendant from him he too suffers from feelings of inadequacy, doubt, and jealousy. These are exactly the kinds of thoughts that arise from the wounded and frightened parts of the self and blot out our connection to our Souls, even if we're in the best of situations. J. K. Rowling depicts Harry's predicament in precisely the terms we are describing, using a metaphor we can understand, and we can see that it's a real struggle for Harry to fight against this force. Eventually he destroys the pendant, and the natural surroundings supply him with what he needs to do so.

What this means is we can look at J. K. Rowling's fictional forests and Oprah's Colorado forest and see something important. Many of Oprah's interviews on *Super Soul Sunday* have been conducted in her garden; "under the oaks" is what she calls this outdoor space. It is not just that she sees Nature as an important resource for inner quiet. It is rather that when we go anywhere and see it with new eyes, with an open Soul, when we allow that quiet to work on us and connect us to the deeper music of the earth—that is when we can tune in to the energy of the Source. It can be a park, your back garden, your grandmother's porch, or anywhere else. What's important is that you come to it with openness and feel yourself as part of something larger.

Nature isn't the only resource, though. As we've seen, for J. K. Rowling a vital creative inspiration occurred during a delay in that long train journey, a time when most people were, perhaps, anxious, upset, and annoyed; and later her inspiration for *A Casual Vacancy* came when she was on a plane. On each occasion Rowling found herself in a space of enforced idleness, where she could do nothing much other than sit back and let her mind be open. It may not have been the experience of nature, or even of silence, but it was away from the usual stressors of her existence. And that was enough. She was away from the ties that life imposes on us.

Anita's experience was again entirely different. She had to move to the very threshold of death, seeing herself stretched out in a hospital bed, dying, before she could detach from the sort of mind-chatter that had kept her confined to the ego-world of her fearful self and kept her sick for so long. Once she felt her Soul, though, she could never again be the same limited and frightened personality as before.

At the core of each of these experiences is one vital element. It is to bring your Higher Awareness to the forefront and to listen. When you do this you will notice that your Soul is speaking to you. The key is to open yourself up to the possibility that it will speak to you. You do that simply by giving it the time and space to be heard. You open up by realizing that you are part of something much bigger than you are.

Each person will have a slightly different way of contacting this place where the Soul can be acknowledged. Some people claim that their Souls speak to them most plainly when they are gardening or when they are caring for animals. Artists of all kinds have told me on many occasions that sometimes simply letting the mind roam free while in the studio will allow inspiration to come from the Soul. In a sense, that is what they wait for all the time.

This all sounds easy, at least in theory, but we also know it isn't so easily achieved as we may wish. For most people day-to-day life is so filled with busy activities that when at last there is a quiet moment all we can do is think about what we haven't yet done. The thoughts keep going through our minds until perhaps we drown them out with TV or some other activity that is outward directed. These are the habits many of us have, and we keep on living like that because we don't know any other way.

How long has it been since you simply allowed yourself to be, in silence? Most of us can connect with the Soul most readily when we are in silence, when we are at peace. There are many ways to do that. Meditation, prayer, being in nature, playing with children or perhaps with animals—those are all ways to align with our Soul because they change your usual way of being. You must find out what works for you. Perhaps you already know, in which case you'll have to do more of it.

Maya Angelou has some excellent guidance here:

When you don't know what to do, do nothing. Don't fill your time with trivia. Simply do nothing. Simply sit. Don't contemplate the flower, don't contemplate this, don't. Don't do anything and you may be able to hear.[49]

Oprah echoes this when she says, "I say the universe speaks to us, always, first in whispers."[50]

It's a good reminder in our busy, I-want-it-now world. Wait until the voice of your Soul speaks to you. It will always suggest something that is, at its base, a loving action. You will know when this happens. It will be crystal clear. Your job is to facilitate the space for this voice to be heard. That means letting go of all judgments and any desire to be right or look good. Allow your inner GPS to guide you to true north. It will show you what you really must do.

What does this look like? Here's an example that may help. A man who lived on his own found his neighbor's dog offensively noisy. It barked at night and fouled the hallway of the building. He was tempted to all kinds of vengeful actions but managed to resist them all. Instead he took some quiet time to think about the situation. Then he allowed himself to feel compassion for the dog and its owners. He began to see that the owners were overly busy people; the dog was unhappy and not fully trained. How could he bring a loving solution to this situation? Then, in the quiet of his being, he knew what he had to do. The next day he went to see the owners and asked if he could take the dog for a walk each day. The stressed owners quickly agreed, and he set a rhythm of walking the dog each afternoon. The dog got its exercise and the man was able to train it to know that it didn't need to bark, and that it shouldn't foul the walkways and halls. The benefit was that the man had a good excuse to take some light exercise himself (something he'd been less than good at), and he came to love the dog. The dog also loved him. In fact, the man admitted later that the dog's love had changed him in ways he hadn't imagined. He found he had more love in him than he'd thought, and his life began to change. The owners were delighted with the arrangement and became more open, eventually forming a friendship with the man.

This isn't a dramatic example, yet it does show just how listening to one's Soul can bring about events that actually do change one's life.

Another very powerful way to connect with your Soul is to express yourself in appreciation or gratitude. It is one of the most powerful things you can do.

Deepak Chopra says that gratitude acts as a form of appreciation for all that the universe has created, and so it "opens the door" to reconnecting with the Source. It is, he says, one of the most effective ways of connecting.[51]

And he's not the only one who thinks this. Oprah urges everyone to keep a gratitude diary in which to record five things each day to be grateful for, no matter how small they may seem. The results are, she says, always "transformative." For whenever we are grateful, and express it, more good things arrive.

When we are grateful we let go of those emotions that keep our minds closed, like anger and sadness. The universe responds by sending us more good things, more opportunities—or perhaps we're just able to see them more easily. When you are in that place you have a much better chance of becoming certain about what you must do in order to fulfill your destiny, even if you are not entirely sure what that destiny is. Your Soul will nudge you to the next step.

Motivational speaker and writer Wallace D. Wattles said it beautifully many years ago: "You cannot exercise much power without gratitude because it is gratitude that keeps you connected with power."[52]

Gratitude comes in various forms, though, and we must not forget that. We find no trouble being grateful for the good things in life—loving friends and family, good food, and so on. But we also have to learn to be grateful for the bad things, because in those unhappy events there is often a profound lesson, and it is that which we must see and be grateful for. We must learn to look at our losses not as things that have been taken away but as opportunities to grow our awareness, to discover our strengths. For example, losing a loved one may be a huge loss. We may mourn and feel inconsolable, certainly for a while. But the more valuable step is to be grateful for all the person gave to life when he or she was alive. This is a stronger, more profound emotion than mere loss. It offers a way to face the future, bringing the dead person's gifts to the light of appreciation, perpetuating the legacy, while grief alone cannot do that.

We have to learn to go with what our Soul urges us to do.

Gratitude will always help us to stay in the present, when sorrow will try to drag us into the past. If we're not able to be fully in the present it will be very difficult to stay in connection with Source. Gratitude always depends upon us not giving in to snap judgments and prejudices. When we even start to think in terms of "what can I be grateful for here?" we stop telling ourselves a pre-recorded story about how we should react to the situation. We stop assuming that it is a disaster or a tragedy. In fact, when we can look at whatever testing and demanding event has occurred we can accept it openly, and it becomes a lesson we can learn from. In doing that we free ourselves from the tyranny of self-pity, anger, and despair. The "value" of the situation is changed for us, even though the circumstances may remain hard. Yet, even in their difficulties, such events will be more manageable because we see them differently.

The world is not going to behave the way we'd like it to all the time, and we have no right to expect that it will. Our task is to look at what arrives and see that it was sent to us as an opportunity to grow spiritually. At that point we can feel gratitude even for the most difficult of circumstances.

Ancient wisdom can help us here, too. Take a look at this quotation from Meng Tzu, a Chinese philosopher who lived between 372 and 289 BCE:

> *When heaven is about to confer a great responsibility on any man, it will exercise his mind with suffering, subject his sinews and bones to hard work, expose his body to hunger, put him to poverty, place obstacles in the paths of his deeds, so as to stimulate his mind, harden his nature, and improve wherever he is incompetent.*[53]

If we accept this, then hardships are to be welcomed, since they can "improve" us and open us to heaven's blessings. "Heaven's blessings" sounds like a pretty good description of manifesting at a very high level indeed.

Occasionally, though, we'll hit a problem. We will be unsure as to whether we're hearing the actual voice of our Soul or perhaps some other voice, "the Imposter." How can you be sure you're hearing the voice of your Soul and not just some clever rationalization?

There's a straightforward answer to this. Listen to the voice you hear and then ask yourself if it will lead on to something more expansive or less so. The loving voice of the Soul always opts for what is more expansive. The ego and the frightened parts of the self always want what is small. To give an example—perhaps you long for a large house with a pool and a mountain view. Do you want it just for yourself? To impress your friends? That's a small vision, designed to make you feel proud of your possession. It is probably not coming from the voice of your Soul. On the other hand, perhaps you have a bigger vision. Do you perhaps want this house because you see you can use this space as a place to gather like-minded Souls who will talk about the things you care deeply about? Do you see this as part of a larger purpose? That's a much larger vision, a more loving vision, and it comes from the Soul.

IN A NUTSHELL

1. An important step in listening to the Soul is to make it a priority to create a space of silence so we can open ourselves to its message, which is always a loving one. It is your job to figure out the best way to connect with your Soul. Once your connection is made your mission will become clearer. The more you open yourself to love, the more your Soul begins to fill your field of awareness and you will feel its guidance.

2. The second step is to feel, as deeply as you know how, the emotion of gratitude. You cannot be simultaneously selfish and grateful, although you can pretend to be! We can feign gratitude when we want to impress others, for example, or to gain advantages in certain situations. Perhaps some of us learned how to do that during those family occasions like birthdays when we had to say thank you for gifts we didn't really want. But behind even that level of politeness there can always be a sense of real pleasure that someone was at least expressing caring. Gratitude has a way of breaking through.

3. Practicing real gratitude will help you to challenge the fearful parts of your personality. Gratitude for what is good—and finding reasons to be grateful for what feel like disasters—will both open your connection to Source. The disasters you survive will make you stronger, and will enlarge your abilities, but only if you allow them to. Look for the life lesson in those events and be thankful for the opportunity to learn. Gratitude will release you from the grip of sorrow, loss, shame, and despair. That's reason enough to be grateful.

4. Practice gratitude. It's the single most important thing you can do.

5. The voice of the Soul is always an expansive and loving voice. It does not want toys or ornaments for themselves but for what they can do for others.

Chapter 7
What Does It Mean to Live in Tune with Your Soul? How Do You Do That?

Since our Higher Awareness acts as the doorway between our everyday ego-based selves and the Soul's ability to manifest our full selves, we have to ask ourselves how we keep that door open. What does it take? And how can we do it?

The words "living in tune with your Soul" don't mean much if we've never had an experience of it or if we've been brought up in a very difficult set of circumstances where love was in short supply, so it's necessary to spell out what it actually means.

There's only one way to be in tune with your Soul, and that is to allow yourself to be vulnerable to others, and love them. That's the "open" part. We do not exclude anyone.

How do we do that? Many ways exist right in front of us each and every day. Drop your defenses and say what you feel in a loving way to someone you know. Take a risk and love those who need it, even if there's nothing in it for you. Trust the goodness in others, even though you can expect some disappointments along the way; then keep trusting anyway. Be loving to someone who can't help you and who may, in fact, forget you ever helped them.

This will get you started.

The everyday model for this can be seen anywhere one sees families and children. Parents love their children and the children love them without reservation, at least when they are young. Yet the parents who are wise know that the child will grow up and not need them anymore. Some parents therefore try to coerce the children into being dependent on them and they give conditional love—conditional on the child doing as they say, being who the parents need them to be. This is very common, but it isn't something that comes from a Higher Awareness. Now imagine loving and respecting someone just because they are human and deserve love, unconditionally, no strings, no expectations.

Can you even begin to think how unusual that is?

Living like that demands courage, for surely there will be those who try to abuse this love. Yet unconditional love does not mean one has to be soft or stupid or childlike. We can love others unconditionally while at the same time recognizing that the other person may need some real help. That's sometimes called tough love, and not many people are clear-sighted enough to know when to use it, and when to refrain.

It is only fear that stops us from being open to the promptings of our Higher Awareness. We're afraid we'll be hurt or betrayed or worse. We apologize for saying what we feel for fear of offending someone, and in the process we become inauthentic to ourselves. Or we simply say nothing and suffer. We do this out of fear. Only when we let go of that fear we can start to connect with our Souls.

Along with this we'll have to learn to listen and even be humble. Be prepared to admit your mistakes and errors. Get used to saying, "I'm sorry" and meaning it when you see you've made a mistake or hurt someone. Admit it if you've done the wrong thing or acted in an unloving way. Then make sure you learn how not to do it again. Tell the people you care about and even those you work with that you love them, and do it frequently in an open, non-threatening way. (I said this would take courage!) Then make sure you do love them, by allowing them to be who they are without judging them.

You should also be prepared to pay attention at all times to what is happening in front of you. You'll see plenty of unloving actions, plenty of mindless prejudice. Notice these acts and decide not to do them. Then find out about how you can help to give relief to those who have suffered, reversing the unloving acts as far as you can.

These are the ways of the Soul.

IN A NUTSHELL

1. Living in full contact with the Soul demands that we allow ourselves to be vulnerable and that we live out of that honest, open space.

2. This takes practice, and courage.

3. It is only fear that prevents us from living with an open and trusting Soul.

4. Without an open Soul nothing much can happen in terms of manifesting.

5. Living by ignoring the Soul's direction guarantees personal isolation.

Chapter 8

Practical Ways to Achieve Alignment with Your Authentic Self

✦———◇———✦

Oprah, J. K. Rowling, and Anita managed to claim their authentic sense of who they are. But how can you achieve this? How can we get back to our authentic selves?

Since this is the core of manifesting—being in touch with what your Soul wants rather than anything else—it's an important question to ask.

For Oprah being who she is was something she discovered early. It wasn't exactly easy, yet she decided this was who she was because that was what ignited her passion. She looked right past all the obstacles in her way and went straight for what she most wanted to do. Just like her, J. K. Rowling made her decision early and wouldn't give up on her dream. She always felt she loved writing more than anything else. She just had to work extremely hard for a number of years before she got the chance to be a writer as fully as she always dreamed. Anita, by contrast, tried hard not to be who she felt she was. Then the violent shock of cancer and a near-death experience changed her. After that she felt she simply could not remain in the state of pretense that had dominated her life until then.[54]

But perhaps you feel none of this applies to you. The three women we've been focusing on have all achieved a level of certainty that most of us can only envy. We can also learn a few things from all this. So, how can we, the rest of us, get back to our authentic selves?

Plenty of people who have considered this question of finding personal authenticity would probably urge us to take up meditation, and—make no mistake—this would be a valuable thing for anyone to try. Yet meditation can be difficult and does not suit everyone, possibly not even a majority of people. For one thing it seems to require an extended amount of time and a regular practice, and many of us have no time or inclination for this. And so the net result is that, whenever the word meditation comes up, quite a few otherwise reasonably open-minded people will tend to say "Oh, I tried that. It didn't work."

Meditation is like the marathon runner's version of self-awareness in a world where most of us just want to do half an hour on the treadmill twice a week. But it's not the only way forwards. You don't have to become a monk and sit in meditation for several hours a day.

Here are some suggestions that you will find will take you back to who you truly are.

Take a good look around you

The first suggestion is simply this—look around you. Do you love your life and the things in it? If you don't—and that's true for most of us at some point—then what will happen is that you'll focus on what you don't like, and will see more and more of it simply because that's where your mind has chosen to focus. As you focus on what you don't like it will become self-fulfilling; you will manifest more of it, too.

You see, when you focus on what you don't like the universe hears only one thing. It hears that you are giving your attention to these unpleasant things. It assumes that this is what you want more of. It has no hesitation in sending you more. So we have to be very careful about what we focus on. Can you find things in your life that you really do love, no matter how small they may be? If you can, and if you can keep doing that, then the universe will register that this is what you are focused upon and it will send you more of those things.

It sounds easy. But really, can you find things that you love? Can you find moments of grace and beauty in your life? You can, but you may have to look hard for them. When your mother or someone close to you criticizes you, can you see that somewhere in that action there is a desire to be loved, to be helpful? That's a hard one, yet people only criticize each other because they feel their way is the best way for the other person—and that is a kind of love. If you can see the love, focus on it. What you focus on will grow. Always.

Try always to focus on the good that exists behind what seems to be bad or destructive. It takes some time to master this, but it is vitally necessary that you do it. Remember, you manifest what you are, rather than what you think you want. If you are sad you'll manifest more sadness. If you're angry you'll manifest more anger. But if you choose to be loving, and give love, you'll manifest more love.

Often we manifest the wrong things because, perhaps, we don't feel loved, and so the universe hears that we are in a state of feeling unloved and gives us more of that. If you can purify your thoughts then you can begin to manifest more good things in your life.

This is why trying to manifest wealth doesn't usually work. When we wish for money we're usually in a place in our lives when we feel the lack of it, so the signal we send out to the universe is, "I don't have enough money." The universe responds to our energy and says, "If that's what you're focused on then that must be what you want, so I'll send you more of that feeling of poverty." That's hardly the way forwards!

This is why it's vitally important to know yourself and the message you send out. If you send out the wrong message you'll only get things you don't want, so it really is up to you to focus on the things you feel joy in. Then more of those things will arrive. Joy begets more joy. And joy can only be felt when you are open to seeing it, feeling it, and living it.

Here are some practical things you can do, every day, to bring your thinking back to the best possible place for manifesting.

Breathe—and know who you are

Breathing. We do it all the time but we seldom think about it much. So here's a short exercise for you to consider. Lie down, relax, breathe. Who could resist that, eh?

Now, pay attention. Does your breathing come easily? Do you find yourself gulping air? Do you breathe through your mouth? Try using only your nose. How easily does the air flow into your lungs and out again?

If you're like most people, the answer is: not very well. We grunt and gasp and the exchange of air is not easeful. Perhaps you have a slight cold, or a cough; something that prevents your breathing from being easy. Notice this.

Why does this matter? Simply because the way we breathe is the most basic way we interact with our world. Do you allow yourself to accept the air and then breathe out the carbon dioxide? Or is it a bit of a struggle? Pay attention to the muscles in your jaw and face. Are they tense? I bet they are. If so, remember, you are doing this to yourself all day, every day, 24/7. Worried about wrinkles? You might want to think about those tense muscles.

The way you breathe is an indicator of the way you face your entire life.

Can you let the energy of the universe flow through you, like a simple inhalation and exhalation? Or is it a fight? And could you make it easier for yourself? Often relaxing will do that for us—yet we don't do it often enough.

The way you breathe will mirror the way you are in the rest of your life.

You can claim easeful breathing, and an easeful life, any time you want. But first you have to notice what you're doing, and, if it's a struggle, you'll have to listen to your body and consciously learn to breathe easily. It's not hard if you pay attention. It's the natural, default position. But somehow, somewhere, most of us have strayed from this. We're like high-speed cars but we've left the parking brake on, and we waste energy stifling ourselves. It's time to pay attention and make a few adjustments.

Take a breather. Change your life.

How do you wake up in the morning?

Think about that for a moment. Do you jump out of bed when the alarm goes? Do you hit snooze? Do you hit snooze two or three times? Do you stagger into the shower, already late, gulp breakfast, and then find yourself waking up only when you're actually on the road?

Now, ask yourself when was the last time you allowed yourself to wake up naturally, slowly, and greet the day. Was it at the weekend? On vacation? Can you even remember? Most of us don't think about this and we don't allow ourselves a gentle wake-up routine, and in the process we fail to claim a real gift for our Souls.

Putting it as directly as possible, the way we wake will determine the kind of energy we take into our day, into our lives. If we wake feeling grumpy, we'll spoil our day and probably the day of everyone who encounters us. If we wake feeling serene—and honestly, how often has that happened to you?—we'll create a different set of circumstances. We'll manifest a different life.

At our core we are happy, relaxed, and serene. That's why bed feels so good! Then just after we open our eyes the cares of the day rush upon us. Or perhaps they've already done so in the form of dreams and have kept us from achieving a decent sleep.

By rushing the waking process we deprive ourselves of a helpful reminder about who we are, about the best version of ourselves. If you can arrange to wake up gently you will remind yourself of the best parts of who you authentically are, and you will be able to carry the energy through your day—no matter what happens. It takes practice, of course, but then everything that's worth doing does.

If we are to manifest what we truly want, we'll have to make sure we wake up and allow ourselves to be who we are, truly. By waking up grumpy, yearning for a different job, a better boss, a win on the lottery, all we do is send out the energy of sadness and neediness. That will only manifest more sadness and neediness. So, notice how you wake.

You may wake feeling energized, or peaceful, or creative, or any number of things. Notice which is true for you. This is who you are.

You can will yourself to be anything at all, but it won't be authentic and so you won't manifest what you need and want. You'll simply manifest what you think you ought to want. And what good is that?

Now, you'll have to be careful about this. If you wake up feeling trusting and loving, that is wonderful. Cherish it. You can carry that energy with you. And you must also be aware that what you are will be tested. The universe will test your trusting self so that you can be made stronger and be purified. People will betray you; and your job will be to see that this is an opportunity for you to be wiser about using your sense of trust. Then you have to continue to trust anyway. So many people are treated badly and then they decide never to trust again. "I'll never trust a man again," said one woman to me about her ex-husband. That's a little like getting food poisoning and then vowing never to eat again. We have to keep trusting, loving, being ourselves—and accepting that these qualities will be tested.

How can we accept these tests? By knowing that each one will allow us to become a more aware version of who we authentically are. Then they are not disasters, but simply facts we can learn from.

So far we have two powerful techniques to help us find out who we are: Noticing our breathing and noticing how we wake. Here is a third.

How do you eat?

Do you grab a sandwich on the run? Do you forget to eat? Do you stuff yourself with a heavy dinner and as a consequence cannot sleep at night? Or do you snack all day on candies?

How you eat is a very strong hint as to how you interact with the world. Do you feel you deserve good, tasty food, prepared with care, eaten at leisure, savored? How many times have people said that they'd love to be able to eat like that, but they never do. When we eat we fuel our bodies; we enter into an agreement with our physical selves to accept what the world offers us and to respectfully transform that into energy. It is a give-and-take agreement we make with the creative power of the universe that has filled our world with good things. Remember, famines don't occur because there isn't enough food, but because we can't or don't get the food to the places it's needed, like Sudan or Bangladesh or whichever place where it is needed.

Can we take the time to consider that act of eating, this most basic of physical functions, and see that it reflects who we are choosing to be? If you choose to fill up on junk food your body will eventually protest. The message you send to your body, and to the world, is that you do not think your body needs good, wholesome food. Your energy, therefore, is that of neglect and carelessness. As your energy is, so shall your manifesting be.

In some ways it does not matter so much exactly what you eat, if you are vegan or carnivore, macrobiotic or omnivore, as long as the food is not a chemical cocktail. What matters is the quality of what you eat and whether you are able to consume food in a way that is calm, reverent, and grateful. If you can do that you are allowing yourself to become the authentic version of yourself. And whatever energy we have determines the life we manifest. Always.

For example, some people choose to be vegetarian because they wish to respect animals or because they want the world's resources to be used properly and they see how wasteful meat production can be. Each meal they take is, for them, a statement of reverence for the planet, a form of appreciation and gratitude. How different their attitude is from that of the person who grabs a burger on the run, dashing between meetings. Whatever we choose to eat, an attitude of respect for the food and for yourself is more loving, and respects the Soul's energies.

If you wish to continue to find out who you truly are, use these three cornerstones—breathing, sleeping, and eating—so you can meet yourself fully. They are primal activities, and so they are truly cornerstones. You may need to keep a notebook and record every day how you breathe, how you wake, and what you eat. This serves two functions; the first is that it allows you to slow down and notice, properly, what you are doing to yourself. The second is that it gives you the space to choose a better, a more harmonious course of action. If you can do this you will come back to your authentic self, and from that energy you will manifest what you need.

Whatever you manifest from this space, be aware that it will be what you need. You may want a million dollars, but, given the huge stresses recorded by those who win the lottery and suddenly have to deal with the wealth, perhaps this is not what you need in order to have the life that fulfills you. Perhaps your destiny is to be a gentle, loving person who guides the lives of others. Perhaps your destiny is to be a person who gets joy from inventing new devices. Accept it if it's true and move with the flow of what the universe provides you with.

The only golden rule here is not to try to be someone you're not, and not to try to do something you aren't fitted to be.

Take a walk

Even a small amount of walking every day will raise your metabolism and increase your health. Human beings are designed to walk every-where. It's only been in the last 100 years or so that we've routinely got into cars and onto trains and buses, and our bodies still need to walk. And so do our minds and Souls.

When we walk a number of things can happen. Our bodies naturally realign themselves and shake out the kinks of the day. This is good. It helps you to reconnect with the physical you, the you who sits too long at a desk and ignores what the body craves—which is gentle movement. When we use walking to come to peaceful accommodations with our bodies we bring more peace into our bodies, and this communicates itself to the psyche, to the Soul. That's one reason that religious devotees of all kinds have so often chosen to go on pilgrimages—essentially long journeys done specifically on foot—because they settle the mind and Soul.

When we walk in nature we tend to notice what else is around us, and so our overactive egos are no longer so able to ensnare us with the worries of the day. This is harder to achieve if you're in a gym, on a treadmill, watching a movie or plugged in to some music. It's really hard to relax into your body under those circumstances. People manage it, of course they do, but it isn't easy, or natural. Walking is the body's way of calming us down and re-centering us. If we're pounding down the sidewalk of midtown, pushing past people to get to our next appointment, we are not likely to feel centered or relaxed—let alone in touch with our authentic and peaceful selves. Even a short unpressured walk will reduce tension, blood pressure, stress, and anxiety. Walking will bring you back to you.

Next time you're walking somewhere, notice how you do it. Do you rush? Do you scurry? Is your gaze fixed on the ground or on the person in front of you? Do you talk on the phone when you walk? Or can you find a way to walk peacefully?

Dancing

Yes, dancing. In our Western world plenty of people are afraid of dancing, most of them men. Cutting oneself off from expressive movement is surely a loss to those poor wallflowers. A little gentle dancing will, if the music suits us, get our bodies moving and encourage us to take delight in that movement. But there is another dimension also. When we dance with others we agree to the basic "rules" of the dance and so we agree to be in rhythm with others as we respond to the music. This sense of harmony with a whole that is greater than we are tends to diminish the ego and its insistent concerns. We come back into harmony with others and see that we are just like they are.

This can't happen if we're eager to show off on the dance floor, or if we're embarrassed to be seen dancing. Harmony comes when we open our emotions to the music, the people around us, and the joy of experiencing our bodies. Next time you're at a dance event, such as a wedding or even the annual office party, notice how you feel about dancing. Most people envy those who find the courage to get up and dance—and yet they hang back and stay at the edges of the floor. The way we choose to dance tells us huge amounts about how we feel about ourselves in public, and whether or not we can be ourselves without fearing judgments. Can you let your Soul be in the dancing, or do you shyly shuffle around the floor out of a sense of duty? Who would you be if you actually let yourself dance freely?

Find a Photo

If you can, find a picture of you as a child, younger than eight, and preferably around the age of one or two. Ideally this will be a picture of a happy child, without adults, although you can select what you feel to be true for you. Place it somewhere you can see it every day, and see if it makes you smile. If you have come from difficult circumstances and cannot find a picture of yourself then feel free to use a picture of someone you know. What's important is to see the happiness on a child's face.

If you do this you will be honoring the Innocent archetype that exists in you and in each of us—the happy, laughing, and unworried part of you that existed when you were very young. This is the aspect of ourselves that we sometimes lose, or forget that we ever had, as we grow. If you can recover the archetype you can rediscover the joy that is at the center of who you are.

A picture of a laughing you is probably the very best one to choose, since when we laugh we are unselfconscious, and totally accepting of the joy that exists everywhere in the universe. You cannot laugh, really laugh, and still be worried about the mortgage, or your job, or anything else. In that moment of free laughter that children have so much of, you can rediscover the generous and loving energy that is truly who you are.

Gratitude

As you begin to check in with yourself more and more often, being aware of your breathing, your moving, your waking, and your eating, you'll find that your awareness of yourself deepens. This is you becoming more real to yourself. Instead of being a person who is tossed around by imagined desires to have something, do something, or prove something, you'll find that you are becoming more grounded in who you are. This is the time when you may want to try the next step of practicing gratitude.

Create a gratitude diary of five things each day you can be grateful for, no matter how small. No repeats, ever.

You'll find this hard at first, but continue anyway. Really, you say, I have to be grateful for paperclips? Why ever not? If they're what you notice, if they are doing something useful for you, then you should be grateful for them, their inventor, their cheapness, or however you wish to see them.

A gratitude diary takes the focus off you and shifts it to other things. If you are grateful then you are, by definition, no longer the center of your own whirl. You are slightly outside it, looking on. If I'm grateful for the help I receive then I realize once again that I'm not all-powerful or all-important, because I needed the help that was given, and it came from a source that was more able/knowledgeable/ practical than I was. I am gently put in my place in the scheme of things. I move from an ego space to a Soul space.

When we are grateful we notice what we like, and when we notice what we like and appreciate we come back to the core of who we are. I may be grateful for peace and a comfy chair and a hot meal. This reminds me that I'm a person who values quiet, peace, and calm space. To someone else this may seem dull, but that's fine. They'll be doing their own thing. And so I come back to me, as you can come back to the authentic you.

I cannot stress this enough. When you claim the authentic version of yourself, whatever that looks like, then your energy will manifest the things you truly need and value. If you work from any other energy you'll only manifest what you don't really want. And say, "Why does this happen to me? Why do I always get more trouble?" It's the way of deep discontent, and I wouldn't wish it on anyone.

IN A NUTSHELL

1. All these actions listed here will bring us back to mindfulness.

2. Breathing, waking, eating, walking, dancing, laughing, expressing gratitude—all will bring you back to the present moment, where you can notice what is truly going on.

3. The question, always, is do you treat yourself in a loving way? You cannot love others fully if you do not love yourself and treat yourself with respect. If you are not acting from a place of love then you're not acting from the Soul, and manifesting cannot happen at its highest level.

PART THREE

Staying in Alignment with Your Soul

Chapter 9
The Power of the Emotions

+————— ◆◇◆ —————+

Remember what the purpose of manifesting is; it is to be the best
version of who you are so you can contribute fully to the life of this
planet. Only in this way can we change our world and nurture peace,
compassion, and a healthy future for generations to come.

Feelings are really your GPS system for life. When you're supposed to do
something, or not supposed to do something, your emotional guidance
system lets you know.

— Oprah Winfrey, Stanford Commencement Address, 2008

Once we've experienced the feeling of being aligned with our Souls, it can be difficult to maintain it. It's a bit like glimpsing a distant mountaintop through trees while on a winding road. Sometimes we see it clearly, sometimes it's obscured, and we begin to feel a bit lost. Fortunately, we have a powerful tool we can use at such times—we have our emotions.

Every emotion that you feel is a message to your Soul. Pay attention to these emotions and use your Higher Awareness to assess them. Then you can elect to respond to the loving emotions and challenge the fearful ones. All emotions are useful and they function as part of a guidance system to let you know whether or not you are in alignment with your Soul. By paying attention to what you feel you can know if you are truly resonating with your Source. If you feel angry and depressed, it's a pretty good sign that you are not resonating with the highest part of yourself and are out of alignment with your Soul. That's important information. It gives you the opportunity to grow.

Feeling is the key word here. Intellectually you may wish to analyze what this emotion means, but you also have to feel it. And you will always feel it in your body, this temporary housing that you have. By noticing the positive and loving emotions you can move into alignment with your Source, and you will experience and therefore understand what Jesus meant when he said: "God is Love and he that dwelleth in love dwelleth in me and I in him." (John 4.16) You will feel the love within your body as well as within your mind.

Notice what is happening to you physically as you go about your day. What are you detecting in the energy centers in your body? (Some people call them chakras.) Your head, your throat, your chest, and your gut are sending you messages all the time. Your body is a finely tuned instrument that will send you physical and emotional information every second, if you pay attention to it. Get into the habit of asking yourself if something feels right.

Pay attention to where you feel tension, notice it, and ask whether this is important information for you. Some people feel tension in their necks and shoulders, for example. If this is you, get used to noticing when this feeling occurs. Then ask yourself what you are doing that makes you tense yourself in this painful way. After all, you are doing this to yourself, although you may be doing it for a reason you haven't fully acknowledged yet. Perhaps it's because what you habitually do is stressful. Notice this. Now, once you've noticed what you're doing tell yourself that you've received the message. You deserve a healthy and balanced body. You deserve to feel right. So you can change this. You can let go of the stress if you wish. Once you start noticing what you're doing and feeling right more of the time, you'll wish you'd done it years ago. You'll be moving back into harmony with yourself, physically and spiritually.

Notice though: this is not the same as "feeling good." A drunk or a drug addict on a high can feel good, at least for a while. Feeling right means that you sense you are in harmonious balance and that your actions, words, and thoughts are loving to you and to others.

In the same way, you can feel whether or not you are aligned with your Source. If there are uncomfortable sensations, then you know a fearful part of the personality has been activated. That means that you are not completely resonating with your Source. You'll have to experience the feeling, identify it, and then arrange to let the fear-filled thoughts go before you can become properly centered.

For example, do you hunch your shoulders in a way that makes you fold in a little on yourself? Many people do. They don't stand proud with their backs straight. This sort of hunch is almost always a way to protect the body, the way a boxer does. Any creature moving into a place of potential danger will be likely to flex its shoulders and move its limbs to protect the vital organs. If you find yourself doing this, if your neck hurts, if you slump your shoulders, the chances are that you are living in fear. Fear is the opposite of love, and it hurts the body. Just ask all those people who take medication for bad backs. Many of them have lived lives in which fear is a dominant feeling.

Again, perhaps you go to the gym and work at getting physically fit. This is good. But then one day you pull a muscle or damage a tendon. Well, accidents happen—and sometimes behind them lie important questions: Why were you working your muscles so hard? What were you trying to prove? Why were you not listening to your body? Were you, perhaps, caught up in an image of who you thought you ought to be rather than accepting who you truly are?

This may sound basic, but it's one of the central tenets of yoga as described by Patanjali in the Yoga Sutras some two thousand years ago. Yoga is a way of watching the mind, so that you notice where you tend to force and where you tend to give up. It asks you to listen, to notice, so you can let go of trying to impress anyone. That's what the fearful part of the self strives to do—to impress others. It's only when we let go of that part of the self that we begin to listen to our inner wisdom. Those are the lessons yoga can bring to our awareness. They are essentially the lessons of the Higher Awareness.

Staying in alignment with your Soul requires you to notice these things, and then it requires one more thing; it asks that we surrender to the positive power, trust it, and do what it says. If you think you can trust it only when it's convenient, or only when your critical friends aren't around, think again. This isn't a part-time job.

Are you ready for that? You might at first balk at the suggestion. I'm not prepared for that, you may say. I want to think about it first! I reserve the right to refuse! This response is only natural.

What you'll discover is that as you begin to hear your Soul more often and more clearly, as you start to live from that loving space and find how joyous and whole it makes you feel, you'll want to take it on full time. You'll recognize that this is where you truly belong. The transition won't be hard at all, but it will take some courage at first.

IN A NUTSHELL

1. Remember—emotions are simply information.

2. If there are uncomfortable sensations or painful emotions, then you know that a frightened part of your personality is active. That means that the part of your personality that is based in fear has taken control. The behaviors of that part of your personality will be things like anxiety, anger, jealousy, resentment, feeling superior and entitled, or its opposite, feeling inferior and needing to please.

3. Aligning your personality with your Source, or what Oprah and Gary Zukav call "Creating Authentic Power," actually means that you are cultivating the loving parts of your personality, the parts that appreciate life, the parts that experience joy, the parts that experience compassion.

4. And once you know that, you know that acting in love will create constructive and beneficial experiences for you, as well as experiences that feel good. Acting in fear will create painful and destructive experiences for you. It's a matter of choice. It's a matter of emotional awareness and responsible choice.

5. Try to find the difference between feeling good and being true to yourself. As Anita Moorjani reminds us, there will be

times when we don't necessarily feel good about things, and "just trying to stay positive" will turn out to be a brave but useless display.[55] Negative thoughts will appear from time to time, and when they do we must be prepared to allow them to pass through. Trying to suppress them or mask them will just make them break out more forcefully. What's important is not whether we're having a bad day or a bad week. What matters is how we feel about ourselves as we go through that day or week. We can feel the feelings, and still trust that the process is ultimately a good one, and that all is as it should be. As Anita says so succinctly, "Honor who you are and allow yourself to be in your own truth."[56]

6. No matter what you achieve outwardly in the physical world, you will not be in your own truth if you are not living in connectedness with the deepest level of yourself. This is what J. K. Rowling describes when she talks about being unemployed and in despair; and yet she decided to go ahead and write her books anyway. She was choosing to honor who she was and is, even while the rest of her outward life was, as she says, "such a mess."[57]

Chapter 10
Intention and Infrastructure: You Need Both

◆————◇————◆

The loftier the building, the deeper must the foundation be laid.
— Thomas à Kempis

One of the most common misconceptions about manifesting is that it occurs in a way that is complete and ready to use. We've already seen that, if anyone has pure intentions and a deeply held vision, then manifestation will happen—that much is certain. And yet that is not the whole of the story. What we want to manifest does not arrive gift-wrapped in a pretty box. What Oprah discovered is that pure intention—which she calls inspiration—and manifesting are actually only the first steps.

Imagine it this way. Say you want to manifest a new car so you can help others to get to where they need to be. Perhaps that's your way of serving your community. That's good. But when that car arrives you know you'll have to manifest the money to keep it running. You'll need cash for gas, for maintenance, for insurance, and you'll need to commit time to this endeavor. You'll also need to be able to park it somewhere safe (which is not always easy in places like New York City for example, where parking can be very expensive). Suddenly you haven't manifested just a car, you've manifested a whole series of expenses and responsibilities. This is what is meant by the terms "intention" and "infrastructure" at the head of this chapter. When we manifest anything from our intention to do good things we have exactly the same concerns. We need to manifest not just the inspiration to use a car to solve a problem but the whole infrastructure that can keep it functioning so we can use it for whatever tasks we have in mind. We need to take steps to make our manifesting sustainable.

This is exactly what Oprah learned. When she first thought about her Network she imagined it in pure terms. She wanted it not for herself but as a way to reach more people so that she could provide "a way to see ourselves differently."[58] And yet it took many long years before the OWN network came into existence, and even then it had a rocky first year. What was going on?

Oprah is perfectly clear about what happened and the process involved. First of all, she says that it's important to have a pure intent, and she is always aware that she is "making every decision flow from the truth of myself."

Specifically, she speaks of her "emotional guidance system" that shows her the way forward. In her Stanford commencement address in 2008, she is absolutely clear about this:

> When you're doing the work you're meant to do, it feels right and every day is a bonus, regardless of what you're getting paid. What I know now is that feelings are really your GPS system for life. When you're supposed to do something or not supposed to do

something, your emotional guidance system lets you know. The
trick is to learn to check your ego at the door and start checking
your gut instead.

These qualities bloom when we're doing what we love, when
we're involving the wholeness of ourselves in our work, both our
expertise and our emotion. So, I say to you, forget about the fast
lane. If you really want to fly, just harness your power to your
passion. Honor your calling. Everybody has one. Trust your heart
and success will come to you.[59]

The problem for most of us is that we can't always be sure what our
gut or our Soul is telling us is right. Fortunately, Oprah expands
upon this advice in a *ForbesWoman* interview. She says that every
decision she makes comes from a feeling of rightness. She asks herself,
insistently, "Does this feel right? Does this feel right? Is this going
to help somebody?" Then she follows this up with two statements.
The first is something that she vowed many years ago: that she would
"only allow my platform to be used as a force for good." The second
statement is a question that she would always ask: "Where do I feel I
can have the most impact or do the most good?"[60]

This sounds very straightforward. Now, let's spell it out. The
steps are:

1. Forget the ego.
2. Check in with your gut instinct.
3. Ask if the action feels right.
4. Ask if this is going to be a force for good.
5. Ask if this is the most effective and powerful way of acting.

This is a careful balance of intuitive feeling and ethical thinking. It emerges finally at step 5 as a way of using those intuitions effectively and working towards a carefully thought-out strategy.

Oprah readily admits that this is not always an easy process and that she had to learn about it the hard way. "I made a lot of mistakes based on emotional giving," she says.[61] The problem is that these emotional decisions may be wonderful, but they are sometimes not sustainable in the real world. Once she understood that, Oprah tried her best to make sure that her charitable inspirations could be sustainable. But it wasn't always easy. An example of the type of challenge she faced is to be seen in the school she founded in South Africa, the Leadership Academy for Girls. She began with a vision for this school, an exceptionally pure one.

Audrey Edwards, editor-at-large of *Essence* magazine, describes it like this:

> *She really believes that this is what her whole journey has been about. That the wealth and the fame and the celebrity has all been about putting her in a position to do this work in Africa.*[62]

This powerful vision of founding a school was Oprah's next step in finding her full potential and expressing it.

She knew right away that a school would need not just inspiration and money but also dedicated employees who could keep it running for many years into the future. The way she put it was this: "You need people who are equally as passionate about it as you are."[63] She was fully aware that the people she needed to work with should be those who knew how to run a school, people who had practical experience as well as passionate idealism.

So what is this idealism?

"It has to start with what you feel most passionate about," she said,[64] and it inevitably comes from the core of your own experience. As we know, Oprah has always said how much she owes to education, and she declares it freely: "I'm passionate about education," because "you have the power to give back from wherever you are."[65] That's at the core of who she is.

So her vision for a leadership academy for girls was absolutely in tune with the deepest beliefs and ambitions she holds. In order to move forwards successfully, though, she needed to work with people who could share the vision and contribute the specific expertise required. That's what she calls "infrastructure," and it has to be built meticulously.

This is the point at which so much manifesting can fail. Oprah herself nearly ran into disaster when a scandal broke about possible sexual abuse at the school. Although she was shocked and taken by surprise, she didn't hesitate. She took the next flight to South Africa and worked tirelessly to sort out the situation, which eventually led to a trial, and finally to an acquittal. Oprah made sure after this event that she had all the necessary resources in place to make certain that such a potentially crippling situation would not recur. She paid attention to the infrastructure because she cared passionately about the school.

Oprah's experience is a fine example of how manifesting works. Manifesting demands that we take responsibility for what we create in very specific ways. It requires that we prepare thoroughly for the next step. Without this, even the finest manifestations will wither on the vine.

The same thing is also true of J. K. Rowling, although in a different form. What we need to notice is that she trusted her deep intuition and left her ego behind, just as Oprah describes. Rowling was entirely determined to write because she knew she had something important to say. What she has to convey is, of course, a deeply moral vision. She sees that the most powerful thing in the world is love, and that this is a vital lesson for children to understand. She also conveys, through Voldemort and the Death Eaters, that ego gratification and selfish delusions have to be resisted. She is one of the few children's-book writers of modern times to suggest that real evil exists in the world and that it's our life task to confront it with courage and heal it with love. That's not the usual content of children's books.

Rowling knew that the best way of taking her vision into the world was in the form of books. It was true to who she is, and how she best communicates.

When the inspiration hit for the Harry Potter series Rowling did not sit around and dream, or complain that it wasn't quite what she'd expected. She got to work, throwing herself into the writing with complete commitment and passion. She finished the first volume, spent time and energy sending it out to agents, and above all else she drew on her expertise as a writer. She had written consistently for most of her life, so she knew she had the drive, the energy, and the personal resources to keep writing these lengthy books for what turned out to be almost two decades. She had prepared herself well and done her homework; and then she got to work.

After the books became successful she took care to surround herself with those who had marketing and publishing expertise, and when the movies were proposed she took just as much care to make sure the directors knew exactly what she needed them to do if they were to render the stories faithfully. She didn't simply take the money and let them do whatever they wished. She found people who truly cared about the way the films would look and how they would say what they said. The same attention to detail, the same loving care, is true of the development of the Hogwarts theme park. We could say that we manifest opportunities, and then we have to work at them.

As we can see, J. K. Rowling followed the steps Oprah describes so clearly.

What this means for us is that to say that dreams come true is not strictly accurate, although many people believe it. Dreams like Oprah's and J. K. Rowling's come true because of an intention, an inspiration that then has to be followed up with hard work and close attention so that the manifesting can be completed.

Anita Moorjani's situation is very much a comparable one. After she started telling of her near-death experience in her blogs and online essays, she found that Wayne Dyer was eager to have her write a book. Anita did not shy away from writing, nor did she avoid the demands of a "public" life. She recognized, in fact, that Wayne Dyer and Hay House publishers were able to offer her the infrastructure she needed in order to make her message of love available around the world. She was both spiritual and practical, and her message has spread as a result. That couldn't have happened if she hadn't allied herself with those who felt just as passionately about what she had to say as she did. The all-important point is that they also had expertise that she didn't.

These three women may seem, at first, to have worked in very different ways. I think we can see, though, that each followed a deep, passionately held intention and then worked hard to make sure the resources were available to sustain that inspiration.

IN A NUTSHELL

1. Inspiration, which is pure intent, comes from the center of who you authentically are. It does not come from the ego. It comes from the Soul.

2. A pure intent is moral and aims to be of help to others.

3. Intents require us to enlist the support and practical expertise of others who believe in the intent as much as we do.

4. When all these elements are in place the manifestation can come to fruition and will be supported fully by the universe.

5. The key words here are inspiration and infrastructure. We need them both working together.

Chapter 11
Intention Is Both Cause and Effect:
Where Is Your Intention Coming From?

✦────── •✧• ──────✦

Intention is the quality of consciousness that infuses your actions.
— *Gary Zukav*

An important question you have to ask yourself when you want to manifest something is this: Where is my intention coming from? Is it coming from my Soul or is it coming from the frightened part of my personality? This is a vital question because an intention is not just a cause—it is also an effect. What you manifest depends directly upon the way you choose your intention.

As we've seen, your Soul is always larger than the self you present to the world. That self is your personality and is somewhat limited. The Soul, in contrast, originates in love and harmony provided by the Source, and so it cares about others and the world. It is the true and authentic you in your fullest expression. Therefore any intention coming from the Soul will have the support of the universe and the Source; that means your actions will be empowered.

If you truly want to access your full manifestation power and want to have the full support of the universe, your intention has to come from this authentic self that is the Soul. This point cannot be made too often. As long as your intentions are coming from anywhere else, you will not be creating from your true highest self; you will not be creating from who you really are and what your Soul really wants for you. Look inside yourself and see where your intentions are coming from. Are they coming from your Soul? Then they will feel loving and they will create more harmony in the world and will be supported by the universe.

If you want to make more money, ask yourself: where is this intention coming from? Is it coming from the Soul or coming from the frightened parts that crave reassurance? Is this money meant to support a good cause or is it meant to satisfy and flatter those frightened parts? If making money is your primary goal, know that you are almost certainly not connected with your Source. This is at the core of manifesting from the intentions of your Soul; learning to distinguish your intentions. Intentions that come from fear within you are always attached to the outcome. So the first thing we need to notice is that we must do what we feel is right and then let go of the outcome.

Here is an example that may help show this. If a friend comes to you for advice you can do one of several things. You can give honest advice so this friend can decide what to do for himself. You can also, if you choose to, give advice that suits your agenda or biases so that he does what you'd like him to. Or perhaps you fall into the trap of just wanting him to be impressed by your ability to give advice. In both of these last two examples, you are attaching to the outcome, and it causes you to falsify any advice you give, even if only a small amount. At that point you are not working from the Source, you're working from your needs. Our needs are the frightened parts of us that want something. If we give in to this fear we will be, essentially, dishonest. Oprah is especially clear about this. She states without hesitation that: "The principle by which I rule every aspect of my life is . . . intention."[66]

What this means to her is she now chooses to make only what she calls "responsible choices"—choices that feel genuine. In this interview with Gary Zukav she describes with real passion how she used to find herself doing all kinds of things to please others, things that she didn't feel were genuine or resonant with her Soul. Then something changed for her when she discovered intention. Pointing to Gary's book *The Seat of the Soul*, she declares: "This book definitely changed my world." What happened was that, once she understood what intention was, she found it was perfectly all right to say no to things and to people she didn't feel aligned with. It was a major turning point in her life. She had suffered, she said, from "the disease to please. Intention cured me."[67]

I think we all know that particular disease. For Oprah, once she knew this, everything in her world changed: "Now I only do what I intend to do," she says. With this intention comes a duty, or as she puts it: "How do we wish to serve our viewers, the public?"[68]

Gary Zukav is completely in tune with her in this particularly revealing interview, where we see an enthusiastic Oprah endorsing what he says completely. Gary puts it this way: "The Intention is the Cause"—the two cannot be separated.

Think of that for a second. This is what we have to get clear, each of us. Are we acting out of intention—which is love for what is good—or out of a desire to please others and look good—which is fear? Which is it? Gary puts this memorably: "Authentic power is developing the ability to distinguish between love and fear in yourself."[69]

If your intention comes from your connectedness with your Soul, that will be the state of consciousness out of which you will act, and your actions will be empowered. Then you are not seeking personal fulfillment through your actions, you are simply enjoying the actions. And when actions become empowered and offer something vital to this world then abundance will flow to you. So, it's a poor idea to think of manifesting money just so you can impress your friends. Think instead of what you can do to help the world become a better place. In that way you may end up manifesting wealth so you can use that wealth to do more good things for the world. It is the purity of the Soul's intention that will bring what you need.

According to Gary Zukav, who is Oprah's favorite author (his book *The Seat of the Soul* is always at her bedside, she says), in order to claim our authentic personal power we must first listen to our intuitions, our interior "voice" in Oprah's terms, and choose responsible actions based on those intuitions. Responsible actions can only occur when we are aware of the emotional implications of our actions before we undertake them, so we have to approach them with a pure spirit. At the same time we must trust that the universe is offering us a spiritual opportunity. This is because the universe is not passive. It is an active participant in our spiritual growth, offering us opportunities all the time.

Gary Zukav is particularly helpful in the way he describes intention. He defines it as a "quality of consciousness that infuses an action." Think of it this way: we can follow an intuition and do something kindly and lovingly, or we can do the exact same action from a point of view of resentment and hate. What we manifest will be determined by the spirit in which the action is done, not simply by the action itself. So the choice of intention is a "fundamental creative act," whether we do it unconsciously or consciously. Ideally we will be alert enough to choose consciously.[70]

One way to help us find our way with this is spelled out by Gary. He describes two steps to the process. First of all, he says; "Go inside; that is [a way of] developing emotional awareness." When we have developed our emotional awareness—the awareness that allows us to see if we're operating from love or from fear—then we can take the second step, which is to choose. At this point we can choose "an intention of love." Each time we do this, each time we decide to work from a place of love, "You become more able to use your capacity in a loving way." In other words it takes practice, and it takes awareness to grow more awareness. It builds on itself, effortlessly.[71]

Gary goes on to say that if we wish to create authentic power we must consciously choose intentions for which we are willing to take responsibility even if we cannot be sure what the final result is. At times we may be afraid that the intentions we choose will lead on to difficult results. Even so, we have to trust and take responsibility for what may happen. Oprah didn't know that her school in South Africa would have a brush with scandal. But when it did she took responsibility. J. K. Rowling didn't know that she'd run into the wrath of fundamentalist Bible sects. Yet, when it happened she didn't back down and she didn't stoop to their level. Anita Moorjani has run into all kinds of criticism, and has responded with loving kindness—and she has not been scared away from her life task. What this means for us is that we have to work from loving intuitions, but we also have to use those intuitions intelligently. This will be different for each of us because our lives are not all alike.

The point to remember is that intuitions don't just arrive complete in themselves. They arrive and we have to assess them to see how to use them. We have to work with what the universe sends us and select the purest intentions only. Then we have to take responsible action. J. K. Rowling had the intuition to write her books, but she didn't just scribble them down and leave it at that. She had to plan them out meticulously, decide on exactly how to write them, and then revise them so their message came through—a message that love is the strongest power there is. If she had simply taken the intuition to write a book and then said, "How can I make a lot of money doing this?" then the books would have been very different, we can be sure. She selected the purest intention, and acted on it, lovingly. That's what Oprah did when she left what she calls "trash TV" behind. That's what Anita did when she saw she had a message to take into the world.

Just as Anita urges us to consider our inner magnificence, so Gary reminds us of a profound truth: "Consider the possibility that you are a powerful, creative, compassionate, and loving spirit."[72] Why does he say that? Because so many of us think that what we do doesn't really matter, and so we don't take the trouble to find our purest intentions. The result is that we manifest, but not at a very high or loving level.

Intention is the cause of manifesting. And intention is always the effect, too. As Oprah so beautifully puts it: "Your intention rules your life and determines the outcome."[73] And the best part is, you get to choose.

IN A NUTSHELL

Four major points emerge here as we are examining the interconnection of cause and effect with regard to intention:

1. For an intention to be powerful it must come from the Soul, not the frightened parts of the personality.

2. An intention that seeks a specific result is not going to be pure, and will ultimately fail.

3. Listen to your Soul, focus on its intention, not yours; act on what you feel and then let go of the results.

4. Intention is the cause and the effect. Always.

Chapter 12

Synchronicity: Messages for Your Soul,
and Messages from Your Soul

+———————— •◇• ————————+

We do not create our destiny; we participate in its unfolding.
Synchronicity works as a catalyst toward the working out of
that destiny.

— **David Richo, The Power of Coincidence**

Synchronicity is a word that means that things happen at exactly the right time in exactly the right way to help you to get where you need to go. Doors that had seemed firmly shut suddenly open. People who were once hard to get hold of are suddenly eager to help. Insights flash upon you where previously all seemed to be deadlocked.

This isn't magic. It's what inevitably has to happen when your Soul is aligned with the universe's will. Anita found, once she was aligned with the Source, that synchronicities seemed to happen around her all the time.

How can we understand this? Imagine a large boulder on the side of a mountain, perfectly balanced, ready to roll into the valley. It can't roll, though, until someone or something comes along to move it. If you nudge it downhill, it will roll easily. It is ready to fulfill its role in synchronicity, to become part of the house or wall you wish to build. Now, if you decide you want that boulder to move uphill you can still do it, but it will require much more force.

The universe works the same way. There are things we need to do to grow spiritually, and so it will make the resources available for those purposes, but we still have to make the effort. It won't do anything without our input. We have to complete the action.

Athletes often report being in the place of synchronicity, or the flow. Those are the days when they feel they can't do anything wrong; everything just slips into place. We know, of course, that the athlete can only do this because he or she has trained hard and worked at the necessary skills, and has the all-important physical attributes to make it all happen. You could say that at that specific time the athlete is fulfilling his or her destiny. If something like this happens to you in your daily life it feels miraculous. And that's the feeling you need to remember, because the message being sent to you is that this is exactly what you are meant to do. That's the message from your Soul. It reassures you. It says, this is not a fluke. This is where you can be all the time.

When this feeling happens to you, respect it. If you feel it and value it, the message that returns to your Soul is that you know you are in alignment, and you know it brings you joy. The universe will then give you more of this miraculous connection to its purpose as a direct feedback.

Artists and poets know this territory. They are famous for saying that the poems or the novels or the pictures they produce came to them, asking to be written, demanding to be made. Leonard Cohen frequently referred to his songs as things dictated to him by his Higher

Awareness, which he then had to write down. Speaking about himself in the third person, Cohen said: "He doesn't have the freedom to refuse."[74] He saw song as something that used him to get important ideas expressed.

Since we are human, we find it difficult to stay in this wonderful place of connection for very long. It's like laughter. It's here now, it feels delightful, and you can't hold on to it if it wants to go. Yet, if we remember what it felt like and how we got there, we can return to it as often as we want to.

Our Souls long for synchronistic connection, and our Souls keep trying to tell us how to get back to that space—yet our frightened selves tend to get in the way.

The important thing to remember is that we can't manifest anything until we enter the place of synchronicity; and when we do get to that space, we can manifest whatever we wish, so long as it is in tune with the needs of our Souls. We can make things happen that are contrary to the wishes of the universe, of course, but this requires us to force those things to happen.

If it's a force, it probably isn't in alignment with the universe. Oprah says about this:

> There is a flow—there's an energy field in the flow—that is also happening with us human beings. We just haven't figured what that is yet or how to channel it. You're either in flow or out of it. If you are in flow . . . it's like flowing with the stream. And the flow is in direct proportion to the center of yourself where God abides . . . where universal energy abides . . . where the divine abides.[75]

She also says, "The answer to the question, 'How far from your center are you?' is: exactly how far out of synch you are in your life."[76]

Let's just summarize the major points so far:

1. You will be guided as to what to do because it will feel authentic and joyful.

2. You must trust this feeling, even if it doesn't look as if it will pay off in material terms.

3. By trusting the process, not the product, you put yourself in alignment with the universe.

4. Now you need to act on what you feel, and trust in it.

5. Ask yourself the question: How far from my center am I? Am I in synch or out of synch with my Source? You may need to ask this often.

Some Examples of Synchronicity

When we look at synchronicity in this way, what we notice is that it doesn't happen in a dramatic fashion. It doesn't seem to happen that someone wakes up to find a million dollars under his or her pillow. Actually synchronicity arrives in small ways—sometimes so small that we fail to notice them until later.

Let's look again at an example we've already mentioned. J. K. Rowling has frequently said that the inspiration for the character and story of Harry Potter came to her when she was stuck on a train, which was delayed for several hours going from Manchester to London—at a time when she had no pen with her! But the initial inspiration sparked plenty more inspirations, and by the time she got off the train she had her main ideas for the novels in place.

The important thing to notice is that she decided not to be bored or upset by the delay, but to follow where her inner voice took her. She didn't dismiss the idea out of hand, even though it was a whopper of an inspiration for an unpublished author. She has even said that until that point she "never thought about writing for children."[77] She accepted the idea, written out of an inspiration, and stayed with the task even though she had no money. Twelve publishers turned her down before she finally found a reluctant taker. And then the books took off. As she said in the same Oprah interview, "It was the thing I was meant to write."[78] It wasn't what she expected to do with her life, but it was the thing she was meant to do with her life.

Now—imagine if she'd simply disregarded that inspiration as being too unrealistic. To this day Rowling is astounded by what has happened, saying she could "never" have imagined the way her life would turn out. The universe has bigger plans for us than we have for ourselves.

Anita Moorjani says something very similar in her book when she points out that synchronicity depends upon what she calls "allowing." As she says: "The very act of permitting without judgment is an act of love."[79] When we stay open and do not pre-judge we allow our essential loving nature to appear, and that's when extraordinary things can come into our lives, including, in her case, spontaneous healing from stage-four cancer. For her it is a case of "allowing rather than attracting." That means she tries always to let the power of the universe work through her, rather than attempting to tell it what to do. In some ways even the name of the Law of Attraction needs to be rethought, because the very word "attraction" will give us trouble if we're looking to understand what is truly going on. It has overtones of us having to put on our best clothes in order to be "attractive" to others, and so it can be highly misleading. Anita sets us right on this; she adds an important piece of information when she says that synchronicities happen "when we love ourselves unconditionally."[80] In that state, when we're doing things that make us happy, when we are allowing ourselves to be truly ourselves, "synchronicities happen all around us."[81]

Each of these examples tells us something important. Synchronicity happens in ways that at first seem insignificant, but later can be seen to be immense. Synchronicity happens to those who are bold enough to take the inspiration they feel and act on it. In each case, the success did not just come "overnight." It came as the result of real trust, hard work, and belief. Moreover, each person's manifesting was true to her particular talents. Oprah didn't manifest success as a scientist; Anita Moorjani didn't manifest success as a painter, and J. K. Rowling didn't manifest success as a musician.

Neither will you. You will not manifest anything that is alien to who you truly are. So you have to find out who you truly are and what you love, and stick to it. If you do, the synchronicities will come. J. K. Rowling didn't think she'd be a children's-book writer, but she knew she was a writer, and had never wanted to be anything else. She just needed a nudge in the right direction. Oprah didn't think she'd be a force for cultural enlightenment, but she knew how to be a journalist and a communicator, and her show was the next step. Anita didn't think she'd become a voice for being authentic to millions of people—but she knew, first hand, what it meant not to be authentic, and she knows she now can use that knowledge productively. In each case these people had to uncover who they truly were, gradually, so the synchronicities could happen.

Let's look at how this unfolded for Anita. Once she began to tell her life story to others, a chain of synchronous connections opened up that led to Wayne Dyer. He read the brief outline of her story she'd written and promptly called his publisher, at Hay House, to ask them to get Anita to write her experience as a book. Simply by telling her story she set in motion events that led to other people making it possible for her to carry her extraordinary experience out into the world—where it could do the most good for others. She had to do her part in order for them to do theirs.

That is what it takes to manifest.

Remember
Manifestation and synchronicity are two parts of the same thing.

And there is one more thing: what happened during the synchronous moments we've described here is that the people concerned did not manifest things. They didn't suddenly find a new car in the driveway. What they manifested was people. The people who arrived were those who were attracted to them, because they were operating at the same level of energy. Like energies always attract. You don't attract what you want, you attract who you are.

You could take a moment, right now, and consider the people you are attracting into your life. For you will attract those who respond to your energy. If you are not happy with those people you presently have in your life, don't beat yourself up. Just observe. And then see if you can raise your own energy, your awareness, in some way. Sometimes just thinking about this is enough to set in motion the change you want. But you have to want it.

Anita is absolutely clear about what this involves. She says that first and foremost we have to love ourselves unconditionally. When we can do that we will bring more love into our lives, as others respond to who we are. When we are with those who we feel are not the people we want in our lives it is because we are not loving ourselves, so we attract other energies, other people, who don't fully love themselves, either. The solution is a spiritual one, and it starts with us. Here is Anita again: "When we live in our true nature of love we'll synchronistically attract the right teacher, book, or spiritual philosophy at the right time."[82]

The objection many people make to the notion of synchronicity is that any phenomena of this sort could simply be a case of the time being right, or of a person being in the right place at the right time. That's entirely reasonable. And it's also accurate, although it's not the whole picture. Synchronicity happens because the universe is ready for what is about to happen, whether it's an alteration in a whole culture's attitude (such as when the Berlin Wall came down) or a point of change in a relationship. The universe works on its own timeline, not ours.

IN A NUTSHELL

1. Synchronicity is not just blind chance, it happens all the time. The very finest synchronicities will happen when we are aligned with the energy of the universe.

2. Being aligned means we have to be ourselves. We cannot manifest anything that is alien to who we authentically are.

3. The universe runs on synchronicity, and we have to do our part to get into step with it.

4. Manifesting and Synchronicity are two parts of the same process. We'll have more to say about this in the following sections.

Chapter 13
Synchronicity II: The Universe Will Send You Helpers

+ —————◇————— +

Though we can't always see it at the time,
if we look upon events with some perspective,
we see things always happen for our best interests.
We are always being guided in a way
better than we know ourselves.

— *Swami Satchidananda*

The most important thing to remember about synchronicity is that it happens when you are in the flow, when you are aligned with the creative energy of the universe, and that it sends you opportunities in the form of people. The people you will meet will be of two kinds, the Helpers and the Frightened. Frightened people will ask you to play it safe and not follow the energy. They'll tell you that you've had the most amazing luck and now it's all over, so don't try anything more. These people may love you and sincerely want to help you, but they are frightened and so they cannot imagine what the future might be, let alone trust that it will be a good future. They will seek to engage with the frightened parts of your personality.

It's the Helpers that we want to focus on. Helpers will always challenge you to keep your eyes open for more opportunities. Each of the three women we're looking at has had these Helper figures in their lives, and each of them has had different kinds of Helper. So, as we go forward it might be useful for you to notice that help does not arrive in the same way for everyone. You'll have to pay attention to see how it works for you.

Let's start with Oprah. Oprah freely acknowledges that she's had many helping figures in her life, from Mrs. Duncan, her third-grade teacher, to Gayle King, her best friend, to Maya Angelou and Gary Zukav. Perhaps the most important Helper—the one she refers to most—has been Maya Angelou. Oprah describes her as a mentor, a mother, a sister, and a person to whom she is, in her turn, a mentor. Their relationship continued to deepen over the many years they knew each other. Oprah describes her as "One of the greatest influences in my entire life . . . a great mentor."[83]

Oprah's Helpers came into her life as a direct result of her social way of relating to the world. We could perhaps see this in terms of the laws of synchronicity, that like energies attract. Oprah has attracted people to her—Helpers—who are at her level of selfless service. Maya Angelou was a communicator, just as Oprah is, and also a seeker after truth. Yet they were different enough so that they could help each other, because they challenged each other to be the best version of themselves they could be, and this way of helping is deep and rare. This is what Gary Zukav calls "A Spiritual Partnership."[84]

We need to focus on Maya Angelou for a moment because the Spiritual Partner is the highest form of the Helper. Gary Zukav makes it quite clear what a spiritual partnership is. It is not the same as friendship, because friends will, very often, only tell you what you want to hear. "Friends don't want to rock the boat," as he puts it. He goes on to say, in conversation with Oprah, that "only spiritual partnerships . . . can help in creating authentic power."[85] What he means by this is that a Spiritual Partner will risk destroying the relationship rather than not speak the truth. Such a person is there to challenge us to be the best person we can be, and will not let us off the hook easily. This is exactly the role that Maya Angelou played for Oprah.

This is much more than just being a friend. In fact, Oprah's very clear about what she has learned from Maya Angelou and one of the strongest lessons, she says, is to say thank you. Here's how Oprah describes their conversation at a time of crisis in Oprah's life:

> *Ironically one of my most desolate moments, barely being able to speak in between sobs of despair, I called Maya looking for comfort and sympathy. Instead she sternly chided me. "STOP IT," she said. "Stop your crying right now and say THANK YOU!" "Why would I say thank you for this?" I said. "Say thank you [Maya Angelou said] because you know God, and you know he put a rainbow in every cloud. The rainbow is coming. Say thank you even though you can't see it. It's already there."[86]*

It's a beautiful statement, a challenging statement; one that asked her to look beyond the present moment to the gift that lies within even difficult times. Only a person of real courage would dare to tell Oprah to stop doing anything. Maya Angelou never hesitated. In that moment she was not being a sympathetic friend, she was being a Spiritual Partner, telling Oprah not to give in to the demands of her frightened ego.

In this way Maya Angelou specifically taught Oprah about courage. As she says, it is the most important of the virtues, because "without it you can practice no other."[87] Courage is not about not being afraid—it's about being afraid and doing what you have to do anyway. Without courage nothing else can last long.

Oprah knows many people, and is known to millions. But only a very few people are at the level of being a Spiritual Partner, and chief amongst these was Maya Angelou. She was probably the most important Helper Oprah has had.

Gary Zukav puts it best when he says that Spiritual Partners come together for the purpose of spiritual growth. Not everyone will have a Helper like this, but some people will. The important point is to realize that such a Helper can be the most challenging person in your life. This may be the person you argue with, fight with, and at times stop talking to. Yet this person may be exactly who you need in your life.

What Oprah learned from Maya Angelou specifically is that we must not allow our past actions to limit who we are now. In fact, the words Maya Angelou said to her about this are words Oprah has repeated, in various forms, on her shows on no fewer than 43 occasions. This was "one of the most powerful lessons anyone can know," as Oprah says. What is that lesson? It's simple: "When you know better you do better."

It's a wonderful message that relays directly to us that we do the best we can, we make mistakes, but we grow wiser so next time we'll do better. It is this aspect of personal growth that Oprah accesses through her friends and mentors and the people she interviews all the time. She seems to gain energy and insight from all the people she interviews, so in that sense they all become Helpers in her life growth. And they, in return, are able to learn from her. Those who receive help are better able to give help to others. That's what happens when we are watching her programs and we, in turn, get the opportunity to grow. That's why Oprah called them "Lifeclasses." As she says, Maya Angelou taught her that this process was a major life lesson: "When you learn, teach. When you get, give."[88]

It wasn't always like this, though. In her early years it was the obstacles Oprah overcame that gave her a sense of empowerment, of personal determination. A Helper can sometimes be someone who opposes us and seeks to harm us, but whose effect is to make us more determined. Only in later years has Oprah's life filled up with helpful figures. Now, as she faces the struggles of the OWN Network, she is still tackling obstacles and accessing the wisdom of her mentors. We see her learning and growing before our eyes. In the process she is becoming an inspiration to us all.

For Anita the situation is slightly different. Her early years were confusing because she felt caught between different religious belief systems, unsure as to who she really was and who she was expected to be. This moved her towards the crisis of her cancer and her near-death experience. The figures that helped her were unusual. She describes how, as she lay facing death, she made contact with the loving spirit of her dead father. She was also aware of the love of her family and of the great strength of the love of her husband. These were, to some extent, the figures who were her Helpers—a tight-knit band of people who were already in her life and whose love was waiting to make itself known.

Anita did have other Helpers, of course. Once she had been through her experience, people came forward to help her spread her story, and of these Wayne Dyer was probably the most influential. Her band of Helpers was less extensive than Oprah's, but every bit as effective. They, too, were people who had the same deeply loving energy she has. Their similar energies attracted them to each other. One could say that her Helper was not a person at all, but her ability to connect with the core of love that is the creative power of the universe.

J. K. Rowling has also had Helpers, but in an entirely different way. Her agent was certainly a Helper, someone who took a chance on her at a time when children's books were supposed to be short, politically correct, and endowed with short titles. *Harry Potter and The Philosopher's Stone* was an impossibly long and cumbersome title at the time, yet Christopher Little knew a good thing when he saw it. He was able to appreciate her energy, and knew what it could do. In this sense J. K. Rowling's agent was a facilitator, rather than a Helper, because he did not alter her thoughts about what she did.

So who were her Helpers? The answer may surprise us. From what Rowling has said, her dead mother was her Helper in very significant ways. This may seem preposterous. After all, Rowling only had the idea to write the Harry Potter books six months before her mother died and never told her mother about them; so how could her mother have helped in any way? A powerful clue exists in the books. We can see from Harry's own yearning for his dead parents, and his desire to live up to their values, that a Helper can be someone who has made an impression that transcends death. This is exactly what seems to have happened for J. K. Rowling. She has said on several occasions that not telling her mother about her Harry Potter stories was her greatest regret in life. This was the parent who had supported her aims all her life, who carefully preserved her first book, *Rabbit*—which she wrote at the age of six. This was the parent whose love gave Rowling a real sense of centeredness, of validation. She was the Helper that asked her to do her best, always. Perhaps this is why Rowling is so positive that the central message of her books is that love is the strongest thing that exists. It is so strong that it can transcend death.

J. K. Rowling's situation seems different because she is above all else a creative person. Her vision is worked out in the process of writing about her characters, and that is a very private space. These characters, based on real people to greater or lesser extents, are the ones who have helped her refine and convey her vision. In contrast, Oprah has grown her awareness through doing the work she has done in a very public way, as a seeker after truth and a communicator. Rowling has sought to reveal a truth she always knew was inside her. Anita found a truth that was revealed to her, all at once, which she knew she had to communicate.

But if we look a little closer we'll see that Oprah always knew she was going to be some kind of teacher, she just wasn't sure how that would work. Rowling always knew she had to be some kind of writer, telling stories to help guide children as they grew. She just wasn't sure at first how that would work. And Anita always knew that love was the core of everything. She just wasn't brave enough at first to live that way. Each woman had to grow in awareness, in very different ways. The truth, it seems, really does lie within us. How it emerges depends on us.

Another Aspect of the Helper

Help can come from many directions, and in forms that may seem at first a little odd. For example, the spirit of a place, of a specific location, can make all the difference to a setting. Rowling's books are all so quintessentially English, it's difficult to imagine that they could have been written by a similarly gifted writer living in a different country. The Forest of Dean is echoed in the forest beyond Hogwarts' gates, and the castles of England seem to be models for the buildings—the resonances are unending. In Oxford in England, for example, exists a school that dresses its young students in uniforms and scholarly black gowns in exactly the same way as Hogwarts in the movies. Since these movies were made with a huge amount of input from Rowling, we may assume that the choices are meaningful. And the name of this real-life school? The Dragon School. England and J. K. Rowling are inextricably intertwined.

Sometimes location is a huge help to the process of manifesting. The point is that our early life experiences are not just geographical. How we grew up is as important as where we grew up. Our task is to use that background.

We could say that Rowling's cultural heritage made the books what they are. All she had to do was choose to use that information so that it could help her. Similarly, we could say that for Oprah, as a rising TV star, the USA was the ideal place for her to be. I doubt she could have achieved what she has done if she'd been a TV star in any other country in the world. The universe gave her an opportunity, and set the stage for her future. She then had to use that opportunity. For Anita the stress of living in Hong Kong with Chinese relatives and a strict Hindu father was just one of the things that allowed her to break through to her transcendent experience. If she'd been in some isolated village she could not have had her near-death experience documented so fully. Perhaps she would have been regarded by many people as, at best, an oddity. She, too, was faced with a choice. It was this: Would she like to come back to this world to finish what she had to do, or would she choose to die? In the case of all three women the universe sent Helpers and helpful circumstances, but in each case they had to grasp those opportunities and face them with courage. They had to see the possibilities that lay within the difficulties.

If you feel your life has no Helpers in it, that it is uneventful or the country you live in is dull, then one way to look at it is to consider that you may not have managed as yet to see how your personal circumstances could help you express whatever it is you have to express. Your background will always help you—if you can see it as helpful, and if you look at it with real courage. Your Higher Awareness can come to your aid with this one, since it can help you to stand outside your usual sense of self.

So when we say that the universe will support you, we'd like you to bear in mind that this help comes in many ways. In fact the universe is already supporting you. Look around at the people in your life. Who are they? Do they help you to grow, or not? Look at the circumstances of your life and ask yourself, has this situation spurred me forwards? Perhaps the current situation you are in is designed specifically to do that, but you haven't recognized that yet? Every obstacle we encounter can become a growthful experience, something to be grateful for, if only we can recognize that help comes in many forms and that not all of them are obvious.

When we begin to notice these things we invite more of the universal energy to enter our awareness, and we can then use it in the way we feel is best.

IN A NUTSHELL

1. The universe will send you help. The most powerful help will come when you are aligned with pure intention.

2. This help will arrive in the form of people who are attracted by your energy and resonate with it.

3. Some people will be your friends, and some may turn out to be Spiritual Partners. Spiritual Partners will challenge you and ask you to see the good in every circumstance. It may not always be comfortable to have such people in our lives, but they will insist we live our truth. Cherish them.

4. The specific lessons we learn from these Helpers are lessons of courage, gratitude, and love. Helpers ask us to reach deep into ourselves to mobilize positive emotions we may not realize we can access. That is their job. They show us we have more strength than we think.

5. Your background will also help you, once you realize it is a source of rich possibility rather than just a series of obstacles you have faced.

6. You have to take the help and opportunities that are offered and use them. Nothing will be delivered to you on a silver plate.

Chapter 14

How Can You Tell You Are in Alignment with Your Soul?

✦ ───── ◈ ───── ✦

When we align our thoughts, emotions, and actions with the highest part of ourselves, we are filled with enthusiasm, purpose, and meaning.

— Gary Zukav

When you are aligned with your Soul—when Source is directing you—you'll notice certain specific things around you that will reassure you that you're on the right path, even if no one else agrees with what you're doing. Here is a list of the signs you can expect to see. To some extent they overlap, but this is a useful checklist you can use.

1. **You'll feel joy**

   The first thing you'll notice is that you have an overall sense of joy in what you're doing, even if no one is paying you or appreciating you. By joy we do not meant the sort of euphoria you see when a team wins an Olympic event. We're talking about something that is deeper and more lasting than that. What you'll find is that whatever it is you do gives you a profound sense of rightness. The writer who cannot wait to get back to the keyboard and the artist who rushes to the studio to begin work are doing it because they feel more alive doing their chosen work than at any other time. Sometimes they lose track of time. It's a deep joy and satisfaction that has nothing to do with results or money. It's a feeling that, here, you feel you are doing what you are meant to. That's what Oprah has said, again and again. It's what J. K. Rowling has said about writing, and Anita has said about talking to people about her life. They feel the rightness of what they're doing, and it brings them real joy.

2. **You'll feel completely ready**

This sense of joy will take on an added dimension because you will feel you've been in training for this task your whole life. Suddenly all those mistakes and errors that felt like such a waste of time take on a new usefulness. The therapist who looks back on a painful time in her own past is now able to see the gift that lay in that experience and use it to help others. We discover that no part of our lives was wasted. It was all just waiting until now to make its contribution. That's what J. K. Rowling acknowledges when she says that her whole life has fueled her writing.

3. **You'll feel confident that you belong**

These two attributes of joy and feeling blessed by your past history cause us to feel that we belong in our world, that we have a right to be here. Perhaps this is a feeling we've rarely had before, yet when we are in alignment we do not feel on the edges or as if we're intruding into someone else's world. We feel we have a perfect right to be where we are, doing what we're doing, right now. Oprah never for a moment doubted that she had a task to do as a broadcaster, and later as a founder of schools, even though she was by conventional standards at the time very much an "outsider."

4. **Synchronicity happens**

As we've already discussed in previous chapters, the universe seems to hand us opportunities in unexpected ways. When we see this it is extremely helpful, of course, and it's also very empowering. It's hard to believe we're headed down the wrong path when the universe keeps giving us so much positive feedback! The synchronicities may be small, but they'll be persistent. Someone will lend a hand just when you need it most. Your computer dies and a friend or colleague lets you have one that was going begging, and so on. Once you notice this kind of event you'll find the synchronicities are everywhere, urging you forwards. So don't dismiss them as luck. They're much more than that.

5. **Synchronicity and money**

Synchronicity will also help you out with money, just when you most need it, and with people who appear when you may be thinking no one will ever come to your aid. Remember, though, that synchronicity does not exist to do your work for you. It exists to help smooth the way so you can work better. It opens the door, but you have to walk through. The thing to remember is that money or the lack of it is not a barrier anymore.

6. **Obstacles melt away**

When you're aligned with your Soul, the inevitable obstacles that appear no longer cause you distress. You'll look at them and feel confident that they will melt away before too long. You may need to be patient but you'll feel calm, knowing that they won't stop you. Think of Oprah with her Network, and all the obstacles that threatened to stop her. She just kept on until the obstacles melted.

If you've noticed some of these things happening around you or to you, and especially item numbers 5, 6, and 7, you can be pretty sure you're not only on the right path, but that you've committed yourself to that path at the Soul level. That single thing, commitment, changes everything. It's like the difference between standing at the edge of the pool looking at the water and actually jumping in. You've only moved a few feet, but the change is absolute, and you feel it! When we commit to a course of action that feels true we set all kinds of energies in motion, all of them helpful. There's a much-repeated quotation that emphasizes this:

Whatever you can do, or dream you can, begin it.
Boldness has genius, power, and magic in it.

This quotation is frequently attributed to the German poet, statesman, and philosopher Johann Wolfgang von Goethe. It was first used by a man called W. H. Murray who was part of the Scottish Himalayan Expedition in 1951—as far as we can tell, it's a very loose translation of something that Goethe wrote as part of Faust. Where it comes from matters less than why it matters to us, here. Murray noticed that making a commitment to one's goal (in his case, buying the boat tickets for the trip) set a whole series of events in motion, including synchronicities and the arrival of helpful people, and he found it absolutely astonishing. He discovered first hand that when you are on the right path the universe does all it can to help you.

You, too, will find yourself feeling committed to your life course.

7. **Feeling centered and calm**

Another thing you'll notice when you're in this space is that you'll feel centered and calm. This feeling will not be derailed by the words or actions of those around you who may doubt your decisions and even your sanity. You'll have a deep knowing that this is what you must do. J. K. Rowling is famous for these moments of knowing—right from the inspiration that struck her for the first Harry Potter story. As a result of this you will not second-guess yourself, because you'll know you can trust your own perceptions.

8. **Sometimes you'll go astray**

There's never any guarantee that you'll make the right decisions all the time. There will be occasions when you go astray. You'll know this because you'll lose that sense of calm knowing that you had before. You'll feel stressed and joyless. The important thing at this point is not to doubt yourself. You'll need to listen to your Soul and have patience that your inner guidance will make itself heard once again. Ask yourself what it was that caused you to go astray. You'll most likely find that you were trying to do something *your* way, rather than waiting for the universe to show you *its* way. That was Oprah, when she was struggling in the ratings game. And when she decided to "take the higher path" she found her true power once more.

9. **Mentors and guides will appear**

As you move forwards you'll find that others notice what you're doing and will step forwards to help you and guide you. These mentors will have noticed that you are aligned and will show you the most effective ways forwards, saving you a great deal of time and energy. But watch out at this point. Some of the people who will try to influence your life will be in it for their own gain. They'll want to take you over. They'll offer you lucrative deals if you'll just agree to do it their way. If this happens you'll know fairly quickly because you'll feel as if you've lost something, as if you've had part of your selfhood stolen or disregarded. So you'll need to listen to your Soul as it guides you back to who you authentically are.

10. **You'll feel physically great**

In many ways this is the best guide of them all. When you're aligned with your Soul you'll sleep better, you'll wake up with more energy, and you will tend to feel better than at any other time in your life. Lethargy, headaches, anxiety, poor digestion, and similar ailments are all signs of a body that is not operating at its highest level, and therefore of a Soul that feels stressed or cramped. The very quickest way of checking this is to pay attention to your breathing. If your breath is labored, or short, or painful, then you are not fully aligned with your Soul. Your Soul and your body know when you're headed in the right direction, and they will become tense and unhappy when you are not. Listen to your body. You have only to think of Anita Moorjani, who was quite literally dying because her ego couldn't allow her to be who she actually is. That's the sort of message the body sends when you are out of alignment. Now, this doesn't mean that all your physical ailments will disappear. We have only to think of the painter Claude Monet, who suffered from such severe rheumatism that later in life he had to have an assistant tie his brushes to his hands. His rheumatism didn't go away. He just stopped seeing it as an obstacle.

11. Your relationships with others will improve

When you're doing what you know is vital for you, something remarkable happens: you stop fighting with others. We only fight with people when we're afraid they're going to stop us from doing what we think we want. When we're doing what we know is right for us there's no point in fighting because we know that no one can stop us doing what feels true. Others may criticize us or attack us, but we know we've got bigger things on our minds. Furthermore, since we have found that centered place within ourselves it's much easier to extend loving compassion to others. For example, a person who has perfect use of all his limbs is not threatened by the possible envy of those who may have physical disabilities, but is in fact more likely to want to extend love and help to those that need it.

12. You'll find yourself being more loving

This arises directly from number 11. You'll find your spirit will open up in new ways, ways that may astonish you. You may discover resources of tenderness and compassion you never knew you had. And as you access this loving part of yourself you'll find it grows stronger. Other people will tend to notice this and respond in loving ways, too, until the world around you is more full of love than ever before. Your world will become beautiful, more beautiful than you believed was possible.

13. You'll feel very grateful to be doing the work you are doing

Gratitude, and a sense of your own good fortune, will begin to fill your awareness at this point. This feeling will come to you mixed with a deep sense of humility. You'll feel blessed, even in the hardest of times that will come, to be able to follow this path. You'll know you're fully alive.

This is not an exclusive list, obviously, but it may well be helpful as you move forwards. Being aligned tends to make people feel more optimistic, creative, and positive. What you feel is often what you become. Optimism will breed creativity, and creativity will generate more positivity. As this unfolds, you'll see that the people around you will begin to notice that you are not as you once were. Some of them will be happy for you. Some may be frightened or spooked. Some—and these are the ones you want to take notice of—will understand right away what has happened. Cherish them.

These are just some of the main signs that you are aligned with your Soul. They exist as ways to keep you aligned. They act as a positive feedback loop that will reassure you and also keep you where you need to be so you can manifest, fully, from the intentions of your Soul.

IN A NUTSHELL

As you move into alignment you can expect to feel and notice certain things happening to you. These are as follows:

1. You'll feel a deep sense of abiding joy.

2. You'll feel ready.

3. You'll sense your inner confidence and sense of belonging.

4. Synchronicities will aid you.

5. Synchronicities involving money will occur.

6. Obstacles melt away.

7. You'll feel centered and calm.

8. Even when things go wrong you'll know that you can find your path again.

9. Mentors and guides will appear.

10. Your physical health will improve.

11. Your relationship with others will improve.

12. You'll become more loving to others.

13. You will be flooded with gratitude for this experience.

PART FOUR

Identifying the Intentions of Your Soul

Chapter 15
Learning to Trust Your Soul: Oprah's
The Color Purple Moment

＋————— ·◇· —————＋

Let your Soul be your pilot

—Sting

"I've learned to trust the wisdom of my infinite self," declares Anita,[89] and it all sounds as natural as breathing. That's because, actually, it is. And it also takes a little patience to reach that point. Trusting your Soul is easy in theory. But in practice you may find that you've taken a big step, given up doing things that have kept you from feeling authentic, and—bang—you don't have any financial security. Your new life isn't materializing as fast as you want it to! Most of us would worry and feel very anxious at this point.

This state of fear will immediately attack our sense of trust.

Remember that old poem:

The boy stood on the burning deck
Whence all but he had fled

In order to live this life you're choosing, you may need to have just as much courage and just as much faith as he did.

An example of this kind of courage, this kind of devotion to a belief, is to be found in the history books when we look at Wilbur and Orville Wright, the inventors of powered flight. The Wright brothers were bicycle makers and sellers, and, because bicycles were hot commodities at that time, they found themselves making a good living. But they weren't that interested in a good living. They were fascinated by flying. So, for several years they took their flying machines out onto the sand dunes of Kitty Hawk, North Carolina, and tried to make them stay in the air. Even when they eventually managed a short flight, in 1903, no one had any idea what the possible future use of these clumsy constructions would be. They were unreliable and fragile, and could only travel a few hundred yards. Everyone thought the Wright brothers were hopeless dreamers.

It wasn't until over a decade later that airplanes began to be considered as in any way useful. The era of profitable commercial flight was still further away. None of that worried the Wright brothers. They listened to their Souls, and trusted there would be a use for their invention. You can imagine their feelings when in World War One all the major powers used airplanes for spotting enemy movements, directing artillery, and eventually as weapons. This must have seemed like a disaster to them.

Yet today commercial flight has proved to be a huge benefit to mankind, shrinking the globe, making understandings between distant nations more probable rather than less. It's now relatively easy for representatives and citizens of various countries to communicate face to face. This has helped to create more peace. The Wright brothers couldn't have predicted any of this. They just trusted their Souls.

J. K. Rowling is absolutely certain about this. Her young wizards have to learn to trust their own sense of what is right, no matter what. That is what lies behind the final struggle for Harry Potter. He has to go, alone, to meet Voldemort and face what looks like certain death. His friends want to hold him back, but he knows what he has to do. This makes for dramatic reading, but it is also central to J. K. Rowling's core beliefs.

You have to stick to what you know is right, no matter what. That's trust in your Soul.

Take some time now to think about occasions when your Soul told you something that you chose to disregard. Most of us can recall times when we overrode our intuitions because of some other circumstance. Can you recall what it felt like when you had that intuition? I'm sure you can recall the sense of gloom that came after everything turned out differently, and you knew you had made a mistake! This is important. This is exactly the way your Soul will speak to you, and this is precisely the way you will feel if you disregard what your Soul says. The longer you disregard it, the worse it will feel.

Our Souls are constantly speaking to us, and we tend not to want to listen. But we can change that. Trust your Soul. It knows more than the conscious mind does.

Perhaps the finest example of how this works is supplied by Oprah when she talks about how much she wanted to be in the movie of Alice Walker's novel *The Color Purple*. It was, as she says, "a fundamental turning point" in her life, one that "changed my faith," so that she was able to see how manifesting really worked.[90]

This is what happened.

Oprah read a review of the novel in the newspaper, and felt she just had to read it. So she went out right away, pausing only to pull on a dressing gown over her pajamas. She bought and read it the same day, and was profoundly moved. Then she went back to the bookstore, bought all the copies they had, and gave them to everyone she met because she felt that it was such an important story. Notice how, at this point, she's following an internal prompting. Her Soul was telling her to act, although she could not have known what the outcome might be.

When she heard that the book was going to be turned into a movie, she just knew she had to be in it—even though she had no training as an actress. She had no idea why she had to be in the movie, she just knew she had to be. Then, one day she had a call from a casting agent asking for her to audition for a movie called *Moon Song*, and was puzzled, because as she says, "I'd been praying for *The Color Purple*." When she got to the audition she saw it was indeed for *The Color Purple*, which was being scripted under a working title. She was very excited. Better yet was that she was auditioning for a major part, Sofia. In the story Sofia is married to Harpo, which is Oprah's name spelled backwards (and is now the name of her studio)—it seemed like a sign from God, or a synchronicity.

She felt certain this was going to happen for her. But no call came. So she waited and waited, and still no call. Eventually she called the agent and was given a rather brusque "Don't call us" response. This was not at all encouraging.

Finally, near despair, she decided she must have failed the audition because she was too fat. So she checked herself into a wellness center—she calls it a "fat farm"—and determined to lose weight.

As she jogged round the track she was in real emotional pain, and she prayed. She told God how disappointed she was that she hadn't got the part, finally adding, "I don't get it, God, but I know you do . . . Please help me to let it go." At that point she felt herself releasing her expectations and her wounded pride, and she simply said, "I surrender." That immediately called to mind an old hymn, and she started to sing it. It begins, "I surrender all," and she felt herself letting go and trusting that all would be as it was supposed to be. At first she still held on to a small corner of her resentment, telling herself that after all this she could never, ever, go and see the completed movie.

Then she began to soften. Finally she was able to admit that she could, perhaps, even imagine seeing the movie with someone else in the role she so much wanted. She sent positive energy to that actress. She wished her well. She let go.

The moment she let go someone came trotting across the track to her and said she had a phone call. It was Steven Spielberg, the director of the movie, and he said to her, "If you lose a pound you could lose the part."[91] She had the part after all.

Oprah's comment about this was that "God can dream bigger for me, for you, than you can ever dream for yourself." God, the Source, the universe, whatever name you want to use for this force, had a plan, and it was not up to her to doubt it or to get caught up in her expectations of the way things should happen. "When you've done all you can do, surrender," she says now, and those words have to do with trust, with letting go of the frightened parts of the personality, and with the conviction that she is serving a bigger purpose than her own needs.[92]

What we'd like you to notice is that in all this Oprah listened to her Soul, and let it set an intention for her. She hadn't seriously thought of being an actress before, but now she did. The Soul's intention that she should be in this movie was not a quiet event—it pushed at her, it made her take action, and, when it didn't come to pass as she imagined it should have, she was in real pain. The lesson for us is that the Soul sets the intention and it's not always comfortable for us to be in that space. In fact, sometimes that's how we know that the Soul has set an intention for us—the idea just won't let us go. It won't give us any peace until we take action. Then, once that intention exists, we have to trust it. We must do all we can to make it happen, and then—let go so that the universe can let things unfold the way they have to. For Oprah this event changed her whole awareness of manifestation; and the movie, of course, changed her life. She didn't change her career and become an actress. Instead the role turned out to be the next, necessary, step in a sequence that led to the creation of the Oprah Winfrey Network. "Your thoughts breed reality," she says, and "when your energy is in synch with what's coming to you . . . you create a space for it."[93] And then it happens.

Notice how Oprah describes this as being "in synch." This is manifesting and it is also synchronicity. Events lined themselves up as they had to, and not the way Oprah had at first wished them to be. Her task was to let the events flow through her.

Anita says precisely the same thing, when she writes: "When I was willing to let go of what I wanted, I received what was truly mine. I've realized that the latter is always the far greater gift."[94] She calls this process "allowing" and she returns to it several times in her book, because it involves that core element of trust that allows the surrender Oprah speaks of. At such times, Anita says, we rediscover the fullness of our own magnificence, that we are one and the same thing as the Source.

This is what it means to trust your Soul, because when you trust your Soul you also trust the universe, since your Soul is tuned in to the power of the universe, always. Our problem as human beings is that we don't always believe that, and so we don't open ourselves to listen to what the Soul is saying, and we get confused and make the wrong decisions.

IN A NUTSHELL

1. Trust your Soul—it has bigger plans than you can comprehend. Listen to your Soul and take action, but let go of expecting specific results.

2. Trusting means letting go of immediate results and expectations. Things will unfold in their own way and in their own time.

3. Manifesting and synchronicity are the same thing.

Chapter 16
How to Stay Connected When We Feel Disconnected

✦———— ◆ ————✦

If you get the inside right, the outside will fall into place.

Primary reality is within; secondary reality without.

— Eckhart Tolle, The Power of Now

Jim Carrey, describing his experiences with spiritual thought at the 2009 GATE convention, was trying to put words to the feeling he had when he knew meditation really worked for him. He felt, he said, as if he had moved through to a world of limitless potential, of love and freedom and light. He felt an "expansive amazing feeling of freedom . . . I saw I was bigger than what I do." Then he frowned and said through clenched teeth, "And ever since that day I've been trying to get back there!"[95]

The audience erupted in laughter at this typical Carrey twist to the story. And yet he's so right about this feeling. When we feel connected to Source it can come as such a surprise that the moment we try to hold on to it, it vanishes. It doesn't seem to respond to coaxing, to bribery or temptation, any more than a wild animal in the woods, glimpsed for a second, would willingly turn around to seek you out. For many people this makes it seem that the connection to Source is unreliable, or illusory—and so they give up.

Yet if you ask any person who meditates regularly, or talk with any artist or writer who can move into that space when in the studio or workshop, or perhaps if you speak with actors who find themselves taken over by what they do—that's when you'll know that being connected is something that comes with practice. It only comes, though, when we practice the things that are authentic to who we are.

That's important to know. We all have different abilities, and so your way of connecting will not be the same as mine. Think, for a moment, of this example—a young man who is a genius kindergarten teacher. When he is in a room of a dozen three-year-old children they are all, just about every day, in a space of contentment, peace, safety, and happiness. How does he do this? He must have had some special training, right? When he was asked what his secret was, he smiled and said, "I have absolutely no idea."[96]

He is simply being himself, authentic and kind, enjoying being with the children every day, and with no real agenda as to how things "should" be. He is unfazed that he is the only man in a facility that is traditionally exclusively about women and small children. He doesn't care what people think, he just gets on with enjoying his work. At such times he's fully connected to Source.

We become connected when we allow ourselves to be who we are, and when we allow the world around us to be whatever it is at that moment, whether it is a world with a crying baby or a noisy teenager.

The trouble with our world is that it is full to overflowing with the things we feel we "should" do. We are all busier than we wish.

Even when we carve out a chunk of time in which we are free we find ourselves filling the space with TV, with shopping that isn't really necessary, with emails and texts and phone apps. So we have developed a mind habit, most of us, that won't allow us to be still, to listen, and feel the connection. As a result most of us experience connectedness the same way we experience sunshine on a cloudy day. Suddenly we're bathed in light. The next moment, the clouds shift and we're in shadow again. The thing we have to recall is that the sun may be obscured, but it hasn't gone away.

It's relatively easy to re-establish connection, but we have to make time to do it. We have to take some time to be still. Anita is worth referring to in this context, because she deliberately refuses to give any sort of recipe for being connected other than feeling unconditional love for oneself and others. Whatever allows you to feel that way, she says, is what will keep us connected. Doing "whatever brings out our passion, creativity, and purpose for living"[97] is what's important. It can be literally anything. One doesn't have to be a poet or a priest. Anita takes care to point out that any life task that we undertake authentically is going to be the correct one for us: "Ultimately, whichever path we choose is the right one for us, and none of these options are any more or less spiritual than the others."[98] The paths will be as individual as the people.

It's not always easy, though. Despite the drama of her near-death experience and being united with the Source, Anita freely acknowledges that even she sometimes feels disconnected. When that happens she realizes she's lost her sense of self. At those times she says she's "not connected with who I truly am, and what I've come here to be."[99] She identifies the chief culprits in her life as TV, newspapers, and other external messages that stop her from hearing her "internal voice." This is the voice of her Soul. It guides her so that she can be who she was meant to be, and so she can do what she was meant to do.

Our inner voice often suffers because there is so much external mind chatter that takes up all our attention, which is a point Anita makes several times. Looking at her own early life in the multicultural society of Hong Kong, which had strict expectations about who she should be, she perceptively points out how she became so confused about who she was: "Listening to all these external voices I'd lost myself."[100] It took a near-death experience to jolt her back to being herself.

Letting go is easier than we think. Remember, it takes effort to clench one's fist and hold on to something. Letting go takes far less effort. Those circling thoughts about what we have to do later are to be left aside. Here is Anita again: "Pursuing what I desire only reinforces separation, whereas allowing means realizing that since we're all one and everything is connected, that which I desire is already mine."[101]

She relays this important information more than once, emphasizing its central value: "When I was willing to let go of what I wanted I received what was truly mine. I've realized that the latter is always the greater gift."[102]

This is absolutely in tune with Oprah's experience with her *Color Purple* movie audition. And a very similar idea is expressed by J. K. Rowling when she describes thinking about her first Harry Potter novel, when she found herself literally hearing words come to her. "The voice said, 'The difficult thing is going to be to get published. If it gets published it'll be huge.'"[103] That inner voice told the truth. Her book was turned down by 12 publishers, and yet it did become huge. Notice, though, that the voice didn't promise anything. It simply said that the next stage would be difficult, in effect giving her a choice as to whether or not she wanted to work hard at getting a publisher. She could have given up. But she didn't hesitate, since, in her words, "this was the one thing in my life I believed in." And in the end she got far more than she could have possibly imagined.

Whatever you truly want is already yours. You don't have to yearn for it or long for it.

If we agree to listen to the voice of the Soul we'll discover that the universe gives us opportunities that have nothing in common with our best-laid plans. Then, we must do what it wants. That's how we stay connected. For our Souls will guide us, if we listen, if we let go of the frightened parts of the personality, and if we have trust that whatever it is we're asked to do is necessary.

Sometimes listening to the inner voice can be hard on our loved ones. Neil Murray, J. K. Rowling's husband, describes how when she is stressed she shuts everyone out and focuses only on the issue at hand in her writing. In the interview he is laughing, with Rowling sitting across from him, also laughing, and he says that at such times she doesn't listen to others. Instead she "trusts herself."[104] Fortunately Neil is now used to this and accepts it, but it does illustrate for us the kind of concentration that is occasionally needed if we are to stay on the path we believe in. It also shows us how others can misunderstand us at times, and how we must not let that deflect us.

There is just one more step. When we feel connected we know it, because things seem to go so well for us. We feel we are in the right place, for one thing. When we know this, we find ourselves operating out of our higher wisdom, and we give authentic responses to situations, even when we're not quite sure where those responses come from. We might choose to leave a job we feel is eroding our sense of authenticity in order to take on a job that everyone else has doubts about. That's what happened when Oprah decided to give up her talk show and begin the Oprah Winfrey Network. At such times we cannot know where our decision will lead, but we have to have faith. If you wish to remain in this place of connectedness to the Source you'll need to be open, trusting, constant in your desire to listen and, above all, you'll need to be grateful.

Gratitude is central to this process, because gratitude keeps us from moving into a place of pride or self-justification. The frightened parts of the personality cannot survive long in a place of gratitude, which is always a place of love. At such moments, even if they are difficult, we'll feel an inner joy that reassures us. It will tell us—you are connected.

IN A NUTSHELL

1. We'll have to let go of outer expectations and be authentically ourselves.

2. This means quieting the mind-chatter that stops us hearing the voice of the Soul.

3. Then, when we hear that voice we'll have to trust it, take its advice, and be grateful for its guidance.

4. We'll know that we're fully connected again because we will feel the joy of being in the moment, doing what feels authentic.

Chapter 17
The Soul and the Material World: Is Pleasure Wrong?

✦ ───── ◆ ───── ✦

So far we've been talking about the Soul and how, at times, it can conflict with the material world. All those wonderful things we see advertised on the TV have a way of feeding the neurotic aspects of our frightened parts. The ads encourage us to feel inadequate until we've bought the product, and so of course at such times we're acting from a space of feeling fearful. When that happens we focus on the material aspects of our lives rather than taking stock of what our Soul is saying.

This leads us to several questions. They can be heaped together as: Why are there so many things to enjoy in this world if we're not supposed to enjoy them? Is wealth bad? And if we're supposed only to follow our Souls, then why were we placed on earth with all these temptations to do otherwise?

These are vital questions, and the answers are not easy. Yet we have to look at them closely. Let us start out by saying that wealth is not bad. Of course it isn't. Wealth only becomes a problem when we focus more on it than on our internal awareness. Sometimes thoughts about money can squash every other thought to the margins. And yet we've all met people, people who may have very little in physical terms but who are generous with what they have, and above all with their emotions. If we can keep hold of emotional generosity and spiritual openness, the money or lack of it is not necessarily a problem. It can be used to help others in many ways. But it cannot do that if it's locked away in some executive's tax-haven bank account.

Our challenge, and it's not a small one, is to navigate along this knife-edge. We need to survive and feed ourselves, but we don't need to become obsessed with that. This is one of the great tests the universe sends us. Can we use our resources well? And by that I don't just mean money. I mean every gift you have that makes you the wonderful individual you are. Can you bring those attributes forward and use them? That's what the wealth question asks. It's a metaphor for the whole of your being.

Can you learn to enjoy the beauty of Nature without demanding that you own a 5,000-acre ranch, just for you? Can you protect the natural environment so generations to come can enjoy it? Can you move beyond the space of "me" and "mine"? These are the real questions.

We've been placed on a magnificent planet and given choices. The choices are a form of temptation, and each one can purify us. We are free to choose anything we wish. That's free will. Those who choose spiritual values will have to go against the mainstream of our culture, and as they do so they will become stronger in their sense of what it is we are here on this earth to do. Through challenges like this we grow spiritually.

Why is this? Think of it this way: when we enjoy the physical pleasures of this world we feel them, fully. They can bring us great joy. And we can get sucked in by them. All of us do, every single one of us. Then our Soul says, there's more to life than this. If that were simply a theoretical question we'd say, "Oh yes. Right. Let's just drop this physical pleasure stuff." It wouldn't mean anything. It would not have been a felt experience. But it has to be felt, on the pulse of life, so that the choice we make is meaningful. If you want to know the spiritual value behind anything, ask someone who has been involved in the physically indulgent side of life and then chosen to move away from that lifestyle. If you want to know what strength of will is then ask someone who has given up alcohol after a life as an alcoholic, or ask the lifelong smoker who has quit. They know how strong those urges are. They don't belittle or ridicule them. They know the power of those addictions—and the craving for physical things is an addiction as much as anything. Our experience on this earth is not a theoretical one, but a practical one based on our physicality.

That's why we have to feel the temptations as they are—powerful.

When we do, when we really get this lesson, something miraculous happens—as we challenge our frightened parts, we rise above the cravings and it turns out we get the physical wealth and abundance anyway. We receive rich and plentiful lives. The difference is we now know how to use them. We use what we have to nurture others. Every gift we give is a spiritual gift to ourselves, too.

Anita Moorjani is clear about this. We are here to enjoy our life on this planet, to laugh, to enjoy the good things, and to have fun with all the delights on offer. She is especially keen on telling us to enjoy chocolate. Chocolate truly is wonderful, but it's an enjoyment; not a reason to live. We have other reasons to live for.

When we enjoy the physical delights of the world we are, in a very real sense, being grateful for what is, and loving the creativity of the universe. This is the lesson that lives on the other side of enjoyment. If we don't feel this, if we miss the point, all we have is gluttony and indulgence. We are here to be joyful, and if that includes our favorite foods then it is the joy they bring that matters, not the food. Life is a banquet, but we can choose to focus on the guests, on the food—or on the joy of being together in beautiful circumstances. Above all else, we are here to express unconditional love, or none of these other enjoyments is going to be worth much. If we don't feel happy and purposeful, the finest meal prepared by the finest chef is going to lack something. If we put joy first, then everything is transformed.

In a slightly different way, the same is true in terms of emotional generosity. The person who will truly know how to look after the homeless will be someone who has been homeless or close to it. This will be the person who can show loving understanding. "Home" is always more than walls and a roof. It is an emotional anchor. The therapist who can treat the trauma victim best will be the one who has lived through a trauma, for exactly the same reasons. From our wounds our genius grows, and it grows so we can serve the world we are in.

Healing trauma is more than overcoming being hurt, it is about feeling whole again. Oprah, for example, wants people to feel wanted and welcomed, because she did not feel either of these things in her early life. She has said this on several of her shows. She has deliberately constructed her shows so that the audience feels welcomed, loved, and acknowledged. Frequently she has given the entire studio audience expensive gifts—on one occasion each got a new car. She had carefully screened them beforehand, without their knowledge, to find out if this was a genuine need for each person. Then she made it happen.

Her critics called this crass showmanship. Actually she was responding to the real needs of real people. A simple, generous action made all their lives that much better. Bringing more good things into their lives helped to transform them so they could run their lives better. It didn't spoil them. It helped to bring them more joy. For Oprah, it's always about more than just the show.

Similarly, J. K. Rowling has spoken about how her mother's painful death from multiple sclerosis moved her writing forward: "If she hadn't died there wouldn't be a Harry Potter."[105] Rowling's declaration that in the end love is at the center of these books exists as a direct connection to the love she felt for her mother. Even Rowling's depression in her mid-twenties was turned to good effect since she used that experience to create the frightening figures called the Dementors, who suck the joy right out of characters' lives when they find them.

We could find multiple examples, but the important point is that the negatives in her life were opportunities to grow spiritually. They turned into positives as they fueled the imaginative process that produced the books. Her books bring pleasure so that her readers can understand important lessons. In her novel *The Casual Vacancy*, she is equally clear that the plight of the desperately poor characters in the book was built directly on her own personally felt experience of poverty, and her wish to let others know the reality of that situation. What was negative has become a powerful driving force in her life.

If her readers experience pleasure as they read, they also learn about the need to accept and support the poor.

This is true for all of us. We need to notice that the negative influences in us will grow unless we get beyond our victimhood and start being generous with the wisdom they can give us. But the Soul can't grow if we're stuck in self-pity. The Soul can't grow if we don't challenge our frightened parts. This challenge is reflected in how we respond to the material world. The material world is to be enjoyed, but not selfishly, not greedily. That's why it's there. Joy always trumps gloom. Chocolate and things like that remind us of this.

Deepak Chopra goes one step further than this. He says that there actually is no material world, since we are Souls. He is right, of course, and Anita agrees with him. The material world is an illusion. Yet it is an illusion that we are living in, every day. The material world could be compared to a video game. The place depicted in the game doesn't exist, but we can operate in it as if it did. The point is that, if the video game is any good, it will allow us to learn lessons about who we are. Unfortunately, as we know, many of the more violent video games seem to teach only violent lessons, but that's the choice we make when we sit down to play them. We choose the game that fits who we see ourselves to be at that moment. If we're interested in anger and destruction then we'll choose a virtual life that mirrors this.

As Souls we can choose a life in the same way. We can choose a life in which we learn about joy and love and peace and gentleness. This is how we can grow as Souls.

IN A NUTSHELL

1. Wealth is not our enemy; it is overattachment to it that is the problem.

2. We can learn about joy from the way we handle our relationship to wealth. Does thinking about it move us closer to greed, or do we elect to move towards joy no matter what our monetary situation might be?

3. We are spiritual beings undergoing a physical experience, and part of this experience is that we have to feel the pull of greed so that we can choose to move towards generosity instead.

Chapter 18
The Soul and Health

◆ ——— •◇• ——— ◆

If we insist on seeing the Soul as separate from the body then this chapter will make no sense. By this stage, though, I think you will be aware that the two are interdependent. If we take the time to realize that the Soul's health is going to be mirrored in some way by the body's health, we have a powerful tool at our disposal. This is at the core of Anita's experience. Her spiritual anxiety and deep fear were, she is sure, what caused her to succumb to cancer; and her move towards unconditional love, including unconditional self-love, is what caused her spontaneous healing.

This is not the same thing as saying that people who are sick have sick Souls. Sometimes those who suffer from terrible illnesses have been able to use the experience to become loving and enlightened beings. Very often, however, we can trace a connection between physical ailments and Soul ailments as the Soul can express its pain in physical ways.

So let's take a closer look at this. We have bodies that have been fine-tuned by evolution to look after themselves extremely well. All we have to do is make sure we treat them decently, allow them rest, wholesome food and drink—and decent air—and these marvelous structures will look after themselves with consummate ease. Our cells will renew themselves without asking our permission, and the body's ability to create its own healing chemicals and hormones is far beyond our capacity to understand. Even a simple thing like a cut finger or a cold will cause the physical body to mobilize billions of the right cells to cope with the problem.

Deepak Chopra, a medical doctor by training, points out that even our skeletons renew themselves every three months. All the cells change and are replaced with new ones. We are constantly renewing ourselves on a physical basis.

So, equipped with this miraculous body, why are so many people so ill? The answer is that we don't always treat our bodies well. We work too hard, we sleep badly, we become exhausted. We eat and drink the wrong things. It is we ourselves who inflict much of the damage our bodies suffer from, since we create environments that are polluted with real poisonous products and residues, and so we suffer.

The way we treat our bodies is analogous to the way we treat nature. We pillage the natural environment for our own short-term gains, and think nothing of it. Many people sport tans, year round—tans they have bought and topped up in tanning booths. They do not think of the damage that is occurring to their skins or the potential for cancer. They want to look good now.

Similarly, in an effort to look good we may take on employment that causes us to be unkind to others in order to reach the top, to "win" the promotion. We may work longer hours than is good for us, living in places we don't much like, so we can get ahead. The body notices all this and sickens. The cliché of "Soul-destroying work" is a phrase that is alarmingly true. Those people who do not feed their Souls in the workplace tend to become depressed. Depression, anxiety, despair, and fear create imbalances in the body's chemistry, and often trigger diseases.

Our bodies are, therefore, exquisitely fine devices that can alert us to what the Soul needs. If we aren't feeling in good health, energetic, vibrant, then there's a pretty good chance that the Soul is tired, too.

This is one reason why we should also try to eat healthy foods, and be careful about what we eat. Too many people in our world are obese, have eating disorders, or consume junk food that makes them ill. This is not a loving way to treat yourself. In each case the consumption of food has not been joyous or an expression of a higher sense of self-respect. The person who guzzles too much food is not, usually, either a happy or a contented individual. Seeking to fill the inner void by overeating is a truism of our times.

If we learn to treat our bodies well, giving them good food and occasional treats, then we will be less burdened by ailments that come from poor or overly rich diets. After all, if you're feeling sick all the time it's hard to acknowledge your spiritual life fully. When our bodies feel good, fit, and well cared for, even if we have physical limitations or disabilities, we vibrate at a higher frequency spiritually, because we are at peace with ourselves. Those who are obsessed with the body can never move fully into the spiritual life they need.

Physical ailments are often manifestations of something we need to address. Back problems and neck problems may, for example, be linked to a life that is too sedentary, with too much time spent at the computer monitor. The body is sending a message—get up, walk around, and enjoy the body that is yours! We ignore it at our peril. Yet there may be another message also, for the person to explore. So, who is the individual who gives you "a pain in the neck"? That perhaps might be a starting place for an inquiry about the ailment as a physical hint. Louise Hay, former president of Hay House Publications, would certainly have agreed that the metaphor is never to be pushed aside. Her bestseller *You Can Heal Your Life* explores this body–spirit connection in great detail. Most illnesses, she concludes, are the physical expressions of spiritual or psychological unease. Anita would agree, since it was her fear of not doing the correct thing, she says, that brought on her cancer.

Our bodies are there to work with us, and to be enjoyed. The body will tell us if we are not living a balanced life. It will tell us if we're not happy in what we're doing. It's a wondrous message system. But it only works if we listen to it.

When the body fails us it is often because we are not paying attention to our Soul-life. The person who suffers a physical collapse because life or work is too difficult is expressing a Soul-sickness through the body. The body then gives us the chance to turn things around.

The hint is clear. Start looking at your body as a source of information about what your Soul needs to do and to learn. It will allow you to find wisdom you would never have been able to access any other way.

IN A NUTSHELL

1. The body is a superb self-regulating system.

2. When the body fails us it is often because we haven't treated it well.

3. Our ailments are very often an expression of what we need to address in our spiritual life. The body is a source of information about our lives that we need to pay attention to.

Chapter 19
The Soul and Humor

———————— ✦ ◈ ✦ ————————

The Soul and humor? Really? Well, yes. Anita is absolutely sure that one of the things we are here on earth to do is to laugh and to love—and in so many ways it's impossible to think of love and joy without laughter. Laughter is the pure element of who we are.

Why is that? When we laugh we express delight in being in our world. We are appreciative and grateful and joyous, all in one moment. If you doubt that, just take a moment and watch a small child or a baby laughing as they play with a toy or a parent. Look at the effect on any adults who are present and you'll see what I mean. There's real innocent delight in such a scene.

Naturally there are all kinds of laughter—cruel laughter and "laughing at others" are just two aspects of destructive humor, humor that is designed to put someone down. These are not genuine laughter. The figures of the smiling Buddha and of the laughing Buddha are well-known representations throughout Asia of this important aspect of the spiritual life, for Buddha is laughing in pleasure at the cosmic joke that is human life.

A life so full of worries, concerns, doubts, and none of them are real—that's what Buddha laughs at.

Real laughter is important because it's not possible to be locked into our world of ego-longing and to laugh at the same time. When we laugh at ourselves we take ourselves less seriously, and that means the fear-based parts of the personality are dismantled, at least for a while. Laughter tells us that this experience, being alive, is fun, is about play, and it's about being kind. It's about belonging to a community, about being "us," and not being just me. Laughter is a sign that we're relaxed, and no real manifesting can come about unless we are in a place of relaxation. Laughter doesn't allow us to pretend to be anything other than we are. We can fake it, of course, but we'll always know we're putting on a show.

The so-called "Laughter Clubs" of India that exist today take as their central value that laughter is a spiritual practice. If you go to one of these clubs you are asked to laugh, even if you don't feel like it. At first it's a force. But before too long the whole group is truly laughing at the absurdity of, well, everything. It's a wonderful way to get free of life's mind traps.

Oprah has always used humor as a way of taking the sting out of difficult topics, making them discussable where previously they may have felt too hard to mention. Similarly, J. K. Rowling has her young wizards learn very early on that laughing at your fears renders them harmless. The Boggarts are prime examples of this. All one has to do is imagine them in a ridiculous way and they lose their power to terrify. When the young wizards are no longer frightened they can easily vanquish their fears. Fear always comes from a sense that one is inadequate in some way. This feeling is most easily put in its place through laughter. True laughter and true joy always connect us with our Source.

We also have to look at a slightly different aspect of laughter, which is what we might call the Jester. In medieval Europe the Jester, or the Fool, was the one person who was allowed to mock everyone, even the king, because his job was to show even the very mightiest how petty and silly they could be at times. It was a dangerous job—as Shakespeare points out in his plays. The same situation exists inside each of us. We have to be able to access that sense of what really is important and we need to challenge ourselves in the same way as a stand-up comic makes fun of politicians today. It's a strong challenge; think of the dictators who have persecuted comedians and you'll have some idea of the way your own resistances may work. Hitler put Charlie Chaplin on his death list because Chaplin mocked him so brilliantly in *The Great Dictator*. When we're able to laugh at ourselves because we know we've been seen through, we can let go of those ego-based ways of thinking about aspects of our life.

Can you laugh at yourself? Can you see your strivings and let them go in that way? This is not the same as giving up what you care about. This is, rather, that we do our best and then agree to let go of any attachment to the results. We can care passionately, and at the same time realize that it's only passionate caring, after all, and it may not be the answer. This is what the Jester has to tell us. He can reveal a new dimension to us when we feel most locked in to "our" way of doing things.

An example may help here. At a residence for children with mental health issues there was an outbreak of food stealing, late at night. The kitchen locks were forced. The management responded by using stronger locks. The windows were then broken open. Bars were placed on the windows. The very next night the thieves broke in through the roof. What was to be done? Conventional thinking required even more locks and bars. Luckily the Jester came into play. The staff got together, thought about it, and laughed at themselves for what they were doing. Then they said—let's just put a good supply of food out openly on a table for those who are hungry in the middle of the night. It's much cheaper and easier than building a fortress. So they put out a good selection of snacks. The problem ended. The residents, who were starting to get angry and oppositional, felt cared for and loved. Greater harmony was the result.

Laughter can cure more than we might think. It can keep our intentions pure.

IN A NUTSHELL

1. Laughter takes us out of our preoccupied mindsets that focus on material things, and so we stop pretending to be something we're not. It is always about being present, right here, right now.

2. Once we're feeling authentic again, we're no longer afraid of anything. We reconnect to love and to joy.

3. When we feel authentic we reconnect with our Souls, and with our ability to manifest. With humor we can never be totally disconnected from the Soul.

4. The figure of the Jester is a useful reminder here, as it will question us and keep us honest. It can help us to keep our intentions pure.

PART FIVE

Manifesting from the Intention of the Soul

Chapter 20
The Soul and Money: Manifesting Wealth

One of the most misunderstood things on this planet is money. We have a tendency to assume that getting it will solve all our problems and make us happy, and that not having it is a source of misery. Daily experience and observation of those around us should be enough to tell us that this obviously isn't true all the time. As long as we have enough to live on, our happiness or lack of it is not dependent upon the size of our bank balance. Yet we persist in this hallucination. What's going on? And what is the relationship of money to the Soul?

This hallucination is only strong because enough people still insist on accepting it, and they accept it because they wish to feel better about themselves and soothe the frightened parts of their personalities. The easiest way of doing that is to focus on money as if it were the solution. It isn't. If I am unhappy I can temporarily reassure myself by saying that I'm doing better than someone else, but that isn't really the answer. It just makes me feel momentarily superior. Since feeling superior means I'm separating myself from others and judging them, it merely keeps me from being fully compassionate.

Real joy, real fulfillment, does not come from gloating over someone else's misfortune, or from comparing our wealth to theirs. Real joy requires us to know who we are and what we are doing to fulfill our Soul's intentions, and that's a little more challenging—at least at first. Compared to that, the gaining of money is an easy option.

And yet we know that some of the finest minds, some of the most elevated spiritual teachers, have also become very wealthy. It's important, therefore, that we look closely at manifesting and money.

Those who set out to manifest money may well succeed in doing it to some extent, but the highest forms of manifestation are not about money. Here is Eckhart Tolle:

> *If making money becomes your primary goal, then know that you are not connected with the dimension, the deepest dimension in yourself that we call the heart. So making money as a goal is not an effective way to live and you will find even if you achieve your goal and make a lot of money, you will find that ultimately it leads to frustration and unhappiness.*

He then goes on to clarify his point:

> *This is not to say that money is inherently not spiritual, that is not the case. It often happens that when your actions become empowered, and contribute something vital to this world, then abundance in some form—and it may be in the form of money—can sometimes flow to you. Because there is such an enormous output of energy into this world through you that the world gives back to you . . .*[106]

In other words, when we become empowered and follow our Soul's intentions, then we may receive money as part of the process, but the money itself is not the important thing. What's important is that the money is there to help us do whatever it is we are doing more fully. Money is a tool to be used, not an end in itself.

Manifestation will provide you not just with money but with abundance. Abundance includes fulfillment, personal happiness, health, and meaningful connection with others as you set about actualizing your Soul's intentions; and it may also include money.

Paulo Coelho perhaps says it most directly, most personally: "What is success? Okay. Success is . . . is . . . money and fame. No. Success is when you go to bed in the evening, and say, 'Oh, my joy! Oh my God! I can sleep in peace!'"[107]

You can't get that feeling if you have chosen not to do the things that your Soul tells you to do, or if you've just worked an investment scheme that nets millions at the expense of innocent investors' life savings. You can only get that feeling when you're doing what you need to do and know that you are doing it the best you can. That's the "joy" Paulo Coelho speaks of. It's a joy deeper than anything money could buy.

IN A NUTSHELL

1. Do what you feel your Soul is telling you to do and the wealth will follow.

2. The wealth that arrives will be there to help you fulfill your authentic goals, your Soul's aims.

3. Real wealth is the sense of joy that comes when one is doing what one feels to be absolutely true.

Chapter 21
Success Is Cyclical

◆————◆————◆

When manifesting happens fully it can sometimes surprise us. In the case of Sarah Ban Breathnach, her book *Simple Abundance* succeeded beyond her wildest dreams. She'd written it from the purest of intentions. As she said in her interview with Oprah, "It wasn't written to be a hit. It was written to be a healing."[108] She was a New York Times Best Seller List author for over a year, and her life as a struggling journalist was over. The money flowed in and she spent it with enthusiasm. She remarried, bought and renovated a house that had once been Sir Isaac Newton's chapel, and she used her money to try to help others.

Unfortunately she didn't manage to hold on to her wealth, and when the royalty checks began to dwindle she discovered some unpleasant truths. Her husband, who had become verbally abusive, had managed to invest her wealth unwisely and had lost most of it. Then one day she found herself standing at the door of her sister's home, holding a suitcase and her cat, knowing that she had nothing and nowhere else to go.

But why did things change? Why couldn't Sarah Ban Breathnach simply stay in the space of success? Why can't all of us do that?

To answer this question we have to look at the nature of intention and manifestation as it plays out in the world. A writer, like
Sarah, may have a pure intention, one that emanates from the Soul,
and so she creates a beautiful Soul-centered book. This book may well
turn out to be helpful to thousands, or millions, and make the writer
rich. But things don't stop there. As Oprah told her in the interview,
one of the great lessons here is that "success is cyclical."[109]

The core of this situation is twofold, and it offers us an excellent way to understand how manifestation works. The first thing to
remember is that we have to be responsible for the good things we
have, and use them well. This is exactly the same as knowing that we
have personal gifts and then arranging to use them wisely. Our abilities, our wisdom, are not "ours" as possessions. They are what we have
as opportunities, and our task is to try to use them for good.

Sarah followed her Higher Awareness in writing a book that came
from the intentions of her Soul. She used all the attributes, all the
experiences she had been given in a positive way, without expecting
any return on her loving gift to the world. That was the first half of
the challenge. But she neglected the other half, which was to make
sure she did not waste her newly arrived resources, in whatever form
they appeared.

Our job is to make sure we use everything we have with care
and reverence, applying our abilities and resources to make things
a little better in our world. This is not a one-shot deal. We have to
keep doing it, mindfully. This is because we grow and we change and
we develop more abilities. We can't sit back and say, "Oh, I gave
my money, or my attention, to that issue when I was a teenager so I
don't need to do that again." You can't do that any more than you

can say, "Oh, I fed the baby yesterday and so I don't need to do that again." We have to remain constantly engaged with the universe and its workings.

The second aspect to Sarah's personal learning was to realize that all success is cyclical. The fact that we are on top of the world today does not guarantee the same thing tomorrow. Professional athletes know this. They know that today, here, in this game or match, they may be the best. Tomorrow, in a very similar game, perhaps facing the same opponent, the opposite may be true. Roger Federer won the men's tennis singles at Wimbledon in June 2012, playing against Andy Murray. Less than two months later, Murray won the Olympic gold medal, playing against Federer in the final. At Wimbledon in 2013, Murray won the title. Federer had been knocked out much earlier. What's also true is that both men knew that one day they would be too old for the game, and nothing could stop that.

Success, the fulfillment of your manifestation, will come, but it will not remain in place forever, since each of us always has more lessons to learn and more things to manifest. Nothing stands still. "The material world is inherently fleeting," as Eckhart Tolle puts it.[110] If we think that our moment of triumph will last forever we are under the control of our frightened parts, and need the reassurance every day that we are still the best. This is the mindset of J. K. Rowling's wicked wizard Voldemort, who always wanted to be the most powerful of them all. His name translates from the French as "flight from death." The only way he can deal with his fear of death is to kill others. As J. K. Rowling says, "he thinks he can make himself immortal."[111] No one can do that. Whatever we believe happens after death, this life is finite for all of us.

At the very end of the Harry Potter series, we are not left with an image of Harry triumphant. Instead, Rowling is careful to show us Harry almost twenty years later, sending his son off for his first term at Hogwarts. The book specifically shows us that success truly is cyclical, and that Harry has used his success, his knowledge, and his experience so that he can give the next generation the best chance at a good and decent life that each is capable of. For Harry it's about a healing that will stretch on into the future. It's an elegant way of saying many of the things we have been discussing here. Oprah puts it beautifully when she says: "All of life is about growing to your personal best. All of life is about growing to greatness."[112]

When wealth and success arrive, they are not the end of the story but the beginning. They represent another, newer, opportunity that asks us what we will do with the new resources we have. How will we use them? Can we handle them? Some people can't. Rock stars and actors are notorious for behaving poorly with their new-found wealth and status. A few, a very few, manage to move beyond that, and develop meaningful lives that go beyond the present day's success. Think of Bono and his efforts to reduce poverty; think of Oprah and her girls' schools in South Africa; think of J. K. Rowling and her involvement in charities to do with childhood deprivation and research into multiple sclerosis; think of Anita Moorjani as she takes her astonishing lesson of life beyond death out into the world. Each is using a gift that has been bestowed on them, and using it not just once but several times.

It's never just about the money.

If Oprah had just been after the money, do you think she would have ever started the Oprah Winfrey Network? The answer is probably no. Her TV shows were wildly popular and commercially successful. She could have moved towards sensationalist TV, or "trash TV," as she calls it, and stayed there for decades, as many of her competitors did and are still doing; but she chose not to. She decided to do what was truly authentic for her. She knew she wanted to develop more meaningful aspects of television, based on spiritual growth. Instead of staying with the old format she moved into the network TV world and continued to explore spiritual issues in a new way. This involved considerable risk, and during its first year the OWN Network lost a huge amount of money—but Oprah was not discouraged.

She speaks eloquently about how she found her intention, way back in May 1992, when having a conversation with Stedman, her significant other. It was he who suggested she could have her own network if she chose. She wrote this in her diary, thought about it, and watched for signs, for opportunities, for nudges from the universe. Above all she was absolutely sure that her intention was true to the core of who she is, her Soul. Here is what she said:

> My goal in life is to live out the truest expression of myself as a human being. We live in a culture that really only responds to that which is familiar, famous, wealthy—people pay attention to people who are known. I've always believed that that was what the fame was for, so that people would pay attention. For me, though, it's been equally important that once they're paying attention, you have something meaningful, worthwhile, and of substance to say to them.[113]

It wasn't easy. This is how the events unfolded.

But as I sat with the idea—own your own network—I thought of the letters OWN, standing for the Oprah Winfrey Network. And I'm always looking for signs, signals, and so I wrote that down in my journal that night, 14 May 1992.

Then in 1998 when Geraldine Laybourne and Marcy Carsey came to visit me with the idea for Oxygen, I thought, Oh, this is the network I was thinking about! Only I thought it was going to be called OWN [laughs]. But maybe I got my O's and my W's mixed up! Maybe it was an X instead! Literally, I thought that. Well, I guess this must be it, because how else am I going to have a network? Obviously, that did not work out.[114]

Now, she sees the lessons clearly:

What I learned from that experience is: Put your name on nothing that you cannot control. Because you need to maintain your voice in all things. That was the great lesson. The mistake I made with Oxygen was that, for me, it was an ego move.[115]

Oprah's great recognition here was that everything, especially mistakes, can be an opportunity for spiritual growth and awareness. Then she kept her intention and waited. This is what she says happened next:

In April 2007, David Zaslav, the head of Discovery, came to me holding an O magazine, talking about the fact that his wife had given it to him and that he wanted to create a channel based on living your best life, because he thought the magazine did such a great job of executing that idea. So I took him into my office and showed him what I'd written in my journal. And I felt instinctively like, Oh my God, so this is how it happens. I realized it was of divine order when he came to see me based upon what I had done in the magazine. He didn't say, "Let's create another Oprah show." He said, "What you're doing is really perfect for a channel—how do we create a channel that helps people the same way your magazine does?" So I said, "Oh my goodness! This is a sign!"[116]

She started her own network—a huge and challenging undertaking—and *Super Soul Sunday* is perhaps the best loved of her new efforts to use her opportunities and talents to their best effect, bringing spiritual teachings to millions.

I think you can see that there is in this an important series of lessons about manifesting. The intention is set when the Soul recognizes the truth of a message it receives, in this case from Stedman. The message could come from anywhere. The important thing is to be open enough to hear. Then, when the message comes, we'll simply know it's the right one. We'll recognize it. Notice that Oprah didn't reject the idea, even though it meant she'd have to work very hard and take greater risks. Her Soul needed to express its fullest capacity, no matter what.

Once the Soul's intention has been set it then requires us to be patient, to pay attention, and to keep the frightened part of our personality in check. Helpers will arrive, but sometimes those Helpers have their own agendas, their own frightened parts, and we have to be vigilant about this. The Soul's intention cannot be forced, and help does not arrive based on our time schedule. It arrives when the time is right, when we are right. The kind of help we get also depends upon the quality of what is intended. Oprah's intent was to produce something better than existing TV, but she goes one step further. She says, "I feel responsible for the energy that I bring into the rooms of every single person who turns on this channel." We manifest, but we also have to manifest with responsibility, considering everyone. Once we have manifested something good our challenge is to stay in that place of doing good things—not give in to trash TV, as it were—and then we have to use our abilities and resources to their fullest. This is an ongoing responsibility.

If we return to the starting point of this chapter, what we can observe is that "success" is often cyclical, and it often requires us to encounter both the ups and the downs of the experience. All of these are opportunities for learning. Sarah Ban Breathnach learned an important lesson the hard way, and communicated it to us in a loving fashion. Perhaps that was what needed to emerge from the loss of her money.

Here is what Neale Donald Walsch has to say about this process of learning:

> You can even be grateful for things that you imagine that aren't any good for you, that you imagine that you don't really want or that you wish you hadn't had to experience. Even in those moments masters say: "Thank you" to life, "Thank you" to God, "Thank you" to the divine self for this particular experience because I know that before too long I will see the extraordinary gift that has been folded into this physical encounter.[117]

By saying "Thank you" we align ourselves again with our Souls. By accepting that success is cyclical we do nothing more than acknowledge that everything has its seasons. Before we can harvest the fruits of our labors we have to dig and sow and cultivate. In the same way each new intention requires us to accept that intention and then to do the work of preparing ourselves and watching for opportunities. We have to weed out the self-serving urges. We have to remain pure in our aims—not thinking about personal gain—and we have to remain faithful to those intentions. Then, in good time, the fruits will appear.

IN A NUTSHELL

1. Success is never permanent.

2. This means that when success arrives we have to use what it brings us in terms of money and status, and use those resources responsibly, for good aims.

3. That means we have to let go of thoughts of personal gain.

4. We have to stay faithful to our Soul's intentions.

Chapter 22
Negative Manifesting and the Wounded Ego

◆———◆◇◆———◆

So far we've been talking about manifesting good things in life. Yet we all know that some people have manifested extraordinary wealth and power through being evil. Think of any of the dictators of small countries who have misused their abilities in order to loot their national treasuries and cause real hardship for others. Equatorial Africa has had more than its fair share of such people. Think of Bernie Madoff, who basically stole millions of dollars using his fraudulent investment firm. Or think of the 2013 movie *The Wolf of Wall Street*, based on the autobiography of Jordan Belfort, who made hundreds of millions from illegal investment trading and eventually went to jail for it.

The best term we can use for this phenomenon is Negative Manifesting. Obviously these people manifested wealth—vast wealth—but we should also notice that they manifested fear, greed, unhappiness, discord, widespread misery, and, in some cases, death. This is the negative aspect of the great power that is the Law of Manifestation. The important point to hold on to is that those with great charisma and great ability are sometimes tempted to misuse those abilities. When they do so they manifest not from the Soul's intentions but from the wounded and frightened parts of the ego—the parts of the self that say, "I want this because without it I feel worthless." What they get, as we can see, is personal worthlessness on a grand scale, crusted over with wealth.

The Law of Manifestation always works. It's a law, after all. The thing we must all bear in mind is that it will give us exactly what we ask for with the core of our being. If we are sad and angry we will manifest more sadness and anger. If we are greedy we will manifest more and more opportunities to be greedy. Our strongest manifestations, however, will occur when we are aligned fully with our Souls, because our Souls are always loving. That is why it's worth focusing on Oprah, J. K. Rowling, and Anita. They have manifested lives that spring from the purest part of themselves—the desire to be authentic and give back to the world.

We must, all of us, take care that we listen only to the positive and loving messages that come from the Soul. Anything else will lead us to misery.

IN A NUTSHELL

1. You can manifest whatever you choose—Positive or Negative.

2. The strongest part of yourself is the loving, positive part that is your Soul.

3. Sometimes the wounded ego overrules the loving and positive part.

4. Manifestation occurring with that energy is always destructive.

Chapter 23
What Is the Definition of Success?
Insights from India Arie and Gary Zukav

Leading on from our discussion of Sarah Ban Breathnach, we need to take a few moments to think about the nature of success. It seems to come very easily to some fortunate people. They seem to manifest everything, effortlessly, right from the start. India Arie is just such a person. A multi-platinum singer-songwriter, she seemed to have got everything anyone could ever wish for by the time she was in her mid-twenties. And then she gave it all up. "I couldn't go any further. I couldn't," she said.[118]

What happened? Success somehow failed to give her what she needed.

India's interviews with Oprah are important for what we're looking at here, because India is now able to say that she had reached a point where she was out of alignment with her Soul. Despite her wealth and fame, she was sick. She had an ulcer, her throat was giving her trouble (which is not great news for a singer and performer), she suffered from skin ailments that seemed to defy all treatments, and she was deeply unhappy. She calls this time her "rock bottom," and we're reminded of J. K. Rowling's description of her own rock bottom—except that Rowling had not achieved any success. Just like Anita and Rowling, India reached a number of conclusions about what was going on. She realized that she had given all her selfhood away to the industry that promoted her. "I would let anyone talk me out of my intuition," she said.[119] Her original ambition, she went on, was pretty clear to her. We could see this as her original Soul intention.

> *Singing in different languages and working with people from different cultures was how I envisioned my career. But in the quest for "success," to make a hit so that I could own myself and then be free, I'd gone so far off the path of my own vision, I didn't even know what that was anymore.*
>
> *I thought the music business had usurped my power, but really, I gave my power away—to other people and to anything I thought would make my life easier.*[120]

India knew she was no longer being true to herself. And that was when she had her epiphany: "I was living the life my mother wanted me to live," she says, and so she was "off the path of my destiny." The music industry was good to her, but "I had what they wanted me to have"—which was not the same as what she herself wanted from her life.[121]

She chose to withdraw from the world, to meditate, and to pray. She elected to retreat to a quiet space so she could find herself again. Her prayer was "to be one hundred percent guided by my Soul"; and then she added the most important part: "Let me have the courage to do what it's telling me."

Things didn't change immediately. In fact, it wasn't until she reached Hawaii and climbed a volcano that she began to sense a real shift. There she began to sense that "we are all interconnected" and that "everything is always going to be OK . . . I was planted with a seed of trust that nothing could harm."[122] This feeling of trust allowed her to let go of all her anxiety, of her eagerness to please others, and of her restless striving. She let go of wanting and started to accept simply being. It was an immense relief to her, a real sense of surrender. She'd found "a sacred space of peace inside" so she could "be in the world and not of it." In this place of not being attached to the material world she saw, more clearly than ever before, that "who we really are is our Soul."

Her Soul, she realized, had tasks for her to do that were not the same tasks as her music industry promoters had in mind. She knew she had a real direction: "fulfilling my mission on earth"[123]—which would require her to listen to her Soul and act on what it told her to do, without second-guessing herself.

I was always told not to get too preachy or esoteric or spiritual. And while I've never said anything I didn't want to say, I've never said some of the most important things I do want to say. About acceptance versus tolerance, and the oneness of all people . . . But now I have.

I've been making my own choices, speaking my truth to the people around me, letting myself be a part of the world again. (Stevie Wonder and Cicely Tyson both told me I needed to break the shell, and they used the same exact words. I know what they meant now.)

I finally reached the fork in the road, and I chose the path of authenticity. I don't know what's going to happen. But I feel good![124]

What India was doing was taking charge of her life purpose by listening to her Soul and then acting in courage. Anyone can lose their way—but it's finding our way back to where we need to be that matters. India now can take that path without fear, because she feels the immense supporting power of the universe as she takes on her life tasks. As she said to Oprah, actually echoing something Oprah had said to her some years before, "the universe really does rise up to meet you wherever you are. I get goosebumps just thinking about that."[125] She knows first-hand what this feels like. The universe will support us, every one of us, if we're working from pure intentions.

Oprah and India's interview was remarkable because Oprah clearly felt that India was articulating her own deep beliefs about what a life purpose needs to be.

In the process of finding her path India reassessed everything. Specifically, she found herself looking at the idea of success in a whole new way. It wasn't about money and fame and another hit record anymore. She'd already gained those things and they'd made her sick and miserable. So she began to formulate her own version of success. It's worth considering it carefully. This is what she said:

"I decided to write down my definition of success, which is, 'Clarity of my intention and reaching that intention while being true to myself and with joy."[126]

She has also said: "You know, what's the point in having it all if you don't feel good? . . . I know what it's like to have millions of dollars and have an ulcer; you can't get out of bed and you can't drink water. You know, it's just like, what good is that?"[127]

All the things we've been considering in the book so far are right here. India specifically waits now, she tells us, for clarity of intention. She has to know that her Soul is telling her to do something that is pure. Then she has to act—she has to reach that intention. In other words, it won't just fall into our laps. We have to be brave and determined and go after it. But, and this is important, like India we all have to be "true to myself." India knows only too well that she can be a commercial success, but she achieved it at the cost of not being true to herself, and it made her miserable. Only being authentic will work. As she told Oprah: "Be clear about your intention and the universe will rise up to meet you where you are."[128]

But how can she be so sure? How, Oprah, asked her, can she be sure she's hearing the voice of her Soul, and not something else? India's reply was a profoundly personal one: "I just know the difference," she said.[129] It's a reply that comes from trusting oneself, and from long experience of listening to one's Soul. Like hearing the voice of a beloved relative on the phone, you just know who it is, even with a bad line and background interference. India prays; she meditates; and she finds that in that quiet space she can open her awareness and listen to her Soul.

The final thing India mentions in her definition of success is the spirit of joy she brings to what she does. She says it in her declaration of what success is, and she says it specifically when she announces, "I feel good."

If whatever you're doing doesn't feel positive every step of the way, it's highly likely that the intention has stopped being pure. Joy is the thing that lets you know you're on the right path. Joy can't be faked. You know the feeling, and nothing else is comparable.

More than this, though, is the reminder she gives us here—manifesting is a PATH. It isn't a destination or a result. It's a series of events that occur along the path of life, and they are characterized by the feeling of joy. You might say that what we do when we manifest is we invite joy into our lives, now and into the future, as we create a meaningful life. That's not "success" as seen by Wall Street bankers. It's something better.

India Arie took a four-year break from her performing life. Presently she continues to manifest songs and she is wealthy, yet what she manifested is not simply "success." What she manifested is her truth, her purpose, and a fulfilled life doing what she feels is important, using the talents she has joyfully. Her songs are loving gifts to the world. She calls it "giving the gift you were born to give." This is a new definition of success, and an important one.

Perhaps Maya Angelou says it best: "Success is liking yourself, liking what you do, and liking how you do it."[130]

If you're truly able to live that way, there's a pretty good chance you're living aligned with Source. And yet, look around you. It sounds like a simple recipe, but how many people can you think of actually live this way?

Seeing success in this personal, interior, way is important for us, too—for you as readers and for us as writers. Our task, all of us together, is not simply to be wealthy and famous. It's nice if that happens, but it's not the point. Our task is to be authentic and do what is true to who we are—and who we are is Love. Only then will we manifest everything we need, through the simple act of joyously following what our Souls need us to do. If we let go of the expectation that we'll be "rewarded" with material goods, we leave plenty of space to see the abundant spiritual rewards that really do await us. A fulfilled life is better than any other definition of "success."

As writers we would define our success in exactly those terms. We're doing what we feel is necessary, what we feel is a good match for our talents, and we're telling the truth as we see it. This is what our Souls seem to need us to do, and that brings us joy. If we were to sell lots of copies the only real reward would be that more people may begin to see life in a new way, a non-commercial way, and so we all start to be a little more humane to each other. That would be a reward worth having! And yet—we already have a reward. It's the joy of telling our truth and being authentic. We are already rewarded.

I know this feeling from my many trips across the US and around the world, screening *The Power of the Heart* and addressing audiences about the movie.

India's interview with Oprah was remarkable for another reason, and that is that by starting her OWN network Oprah too took a risk, rather like the one India took when she stopped performing. The new network consumed a lot of time and energy and money, with no guarantee of a quick reward. Why would Oprah do that? She could have chosen to retire. She had enough money. So did India. Instead they both elected to do what felt true to who they are. For Oprah, particularly, it is her life mission that is important. She feels that same burning fire to be an educator that she always did, and being able to follow her mission is success—whether or not the money rolls in. It's a success beyond the ordinary definitions of "success." It's a spiritual definition. Here is what Eckart Tolle says about this: "Some changes look negative on the surface but you will soon realize that space is being created in your life for something new to emerge."[131]

Gary Zukav would take this one step further, since he sees the very words "success" and "failure" as words created to explain what we do to ourselves, merely in physical terms. "Success and failure are only meaningful within a certain arena—within the Earthschool,"[132] he says. They do not correspond to the spiritual world, and he suggests a better way forwards: "Give up altogether looking at your experience as success or failure" because "you cannot know how the universe works."[133]

He is right. No one can know exactly how the universe works, because as humans we simply can't comprehend concepts that big. So ultimately it is impossible to say that someone's life is successful or not, since we do not know what the ultimate effects of that life may be. Dr. Martin Luther King Jr. was assassinated before he'd achieved equality for African Americans in the USA, but that does not mean he wasted his life. His legacy continues. In India, Mohandas (Mahatma) Gandhi was assassinated at a crucial political moment in the country's history. Yet the results of his life's work continue today. The same is true of all our lives. We simply do not know what we have set in motion or how it will end. Quoting Baba Meher, Gary Zukav repeats the important phrase that most of us only know one half of: "Do your best; don't worry; be happy." Notice that key section, "Do your best." We have work to do, and it must be our best effort. Then we have to let go of the result. That result includes all judgments of success or failure. As Gary Zukav says: "There is no such thing as failure . . . the universe does not judge you."[134]

Doing your best is its own reward.

IN A NUTSHELL

1. Sometimes manifesting "success" comes with crippling pressures.

2. Real success is doing what you feel is true to your Soul.

3. Real success involves joy and giving back.

4. Success itself is an illusion since we cannot judge what the result of anyone's life might be.

5. We must always do our best and then let go of expectations of rewards.

Chapter 24
The Purpose of Trials

———— ◆ · ◇ · ◆ ————

When we long for life without difficulties, remind us that oaks grow strong in contrary winds and diamonds are made under pressure.
— **Peter Marshall**

I cannot praise a fugitive and cloister'd virtue
— *John Milton*

Even though we now know that success is definitely cyclical, when those downturns occur they can be extremely unsettling.

No one knows this better than Oprah because, as we have noticed, when she decided to launch her OWN Network in 2011 she ran into some daunting obstacles almost immediately. Her ratings were low and the press went after her, filling the media with negative reports. And then things got worse. "I don't know of a worse week of my entire life," Oprah said, thinking of the difficult decisions she had to make in March 2012 that caused her to lay off 30 of her staff and cancel the much-anticipated *Rosie O'Donnell Show*.[135] It seemed as if everyone was eager for a chance to criticize her fledgling organization. The same news organizations that had once adored her were now

216

reporting only bad news. She felt as if the media were "lying in wait" for her, hungering for her to fail.

She could have responded to this in a variety of ways, but what is remarkable is how she was able to see the lesson behind the event. As she said, "when the winds of change come" the important question to ask is: "What does this really mean?"[136]

She saw right away that this was a "spiritual trial," one that was going to be helpful to her if she paid attention. She didn't see the events as humiliating. Rather she saw that they allowed her to have a new perspective on who she truly was. "You can't know who you are if you spend too much time on the mountain top," she said. "You have to be taken down from the mountain so you can rise to the next level."[137]

This is the vital center of the experience.

Seen this way, her experience became a powerful lesson about life and manifesting. Oprah describes its spiritual quality beautifully: "All trial does is it brings you closer to the center of the source of who you are."[138] She didn't give up. Instead she reaffirmed her commitment to her inner vision about what a network could be. That's what it means to be brought to the center of one's Source—it means contacting one's Soul. As she did so she reconnected with her initial reasons for becoming the person she is. She'd always wanted to be part of "transforming people's lives"; now she had to ask, "was this the right path?" She hadn't deviated from her desire to use television for "information and enlightenment" one bit. She'd simply deepened her resolve.

Fortunately Oprah is blessed with persistence and courage. In fact she calls herself "persistent to the point of resilience." And so she set about making her vision work. Along the way she knew she had the support of the universe, feeling it in what she describes as those "all-will-be-well moments" that would come along, reassuring her.[139] The most powerful of these she calls her "*Color Purple* moments"—referring back to her audition for the movie, which worked out only when she surrendered to the will of the universe. It's an experience she has never forgotten. "A *Color Purple* moment . . . is when things break open for you and you are exactly where you need to be,"[140] she explains. It's a deeply intuitive feeling that, no matter what anyone else thinks, this is where you need to be, right now. She saw her best friend, Gayle King, leave her network and take a job as a news anchor with CBS, and realized that, even though they'd worked together for years and been best friends since first grade, this was something Gayle needed to do. Oprah didn't hang on to the past or expect the present to remain the way she wanted it to be. She let go and saw that it all was working out perfectly, the way it was supposed to. That was a *Color Purple* moment.

Knowing this, Oprah stayed with her vision and on 18 June 2012 she received word that *Super Soul Sunday* had won an Emmy for daytime TV. It was a vindication of all she'd been trying to do. She might not have won the ratings war yet, but she was being recognized for quality broadcasting, which matters far more to her. The way Oprah reacted to the news is also interesting, and important for our discussion. After she'd felt the triumph and enjoyed the success, the hugs and handshakes, she moved into a place of profound gratitude—even after all the trials she'd been through.

"Who gets to do this?" she said, with wonder in her voice at how fortunate she was to be able to follow her dream. "Wow. That's grace. That's good."[141]

Trials are spiritual opportunities that allow us to reconnect with our truest motivations for what we're doing. If we cannot reconnect, we're probably doing things for the wrong reasons. Oprah knew what she was going through and found the lesson in it—a spiritual lesson: "I will move through life differently, enhanced by that experience" is how she phrases it.[142] It wasn't easy; it was a growth point for her Soul.

Oprah's experience of a life trial is the strongest example of this—partly because she's been so open about her life. It doesn't take a huge amount of effort, though, for us to connect this to J. K. Rowling's despair as a penniless single mother, deciding that she was just going to go ahead and write her stories anyway. And surely it must remind us of Sarah Ban Breathnach's experience of gaining wealth and then losing it almost as rapidly. For Anita the trial is every day in front of her. Even though she has now moved into a new relationship with herself and a new alignment with her Soul, we can be quite sure that each day offers challenges in which she could, if she chose, slip back into the way of being that made her sick to begin with.

Every trial is a spiritual one. Every one is an opportunity to become more aligned with your Soul. Perhaps the essence of it can be summed up as this—If you put your relationship to your Soul first, then the Soul will work everything else out.

IN A NUTSHELL

1. Every trial is an opportunity for spiritual development. Oppositions ask us to learn more about trusting our Souls.

2. We must put our relationship to our Soul first, always.

3. The Soul will not lead you astray.

Chapter 25
Manifesting and the Unconscious

＋————◆◇◆————＋

This is in many ways the most difficult part of manifesting because it is the hardest to pin down. The core of it is that we manifest what we want in our Souls, but sometimes our Unconscious self doesn't want the same thing as our conscious self. So, it's safe to say that almost everyone's Soul wants peace, happiness, and health. Yet we know that most people don't manifest that.

What happens is that somewhere deep inside ourselves, in the Unconscious, we don't actually believe we deserve the good things we say we want. We don't love ourselves or believe that good things can happen to us.

Understanding this phenomenon can be helpful if we wish to free ourselves from those unconsciously held beliefs.

This is how it works: we take in messages and images when we're very young. Some of those messages aren't helpful. So the child who has been mistreated may have internalized the sense that "bad things happen to me." This child wants to be happy, but there's a large and powerful part of the psyche that says: "It'll never happen for you! It never did when you were small!" This is the voice of learned experience, based in past events. This is the wounded part of the frightened ego. Unless the child can notice this and then seek to change this internal sense, what he or she will manifest is a lifetime of repeated disappointments and despair. After all, that's what the past has always brought. We can see this every day. Many children will give up at something—school, sports, trying to be helpful, being loving—at a surprisingly early age. What this tells us is that the Unconscious is sufficiently strong that it will override the Soul— unless we take care that it doesn't.

So the man who has a gift as a teacher, but who had a disrupted childhood spent in many different temporary homes, may well decide that he wants to stay in one place and simply stop moving. While he is operating out of this wounded sense of self he may feel temporarily better. He carries this desire for peace and stasis deep in his Unconscious. But his Soul knows he has a gift he's not using fully, and so depression is bound to set in after a while. He has a choice: to listen to his Soul, which calls on him to go out, travel, and be a teacher of great ideas, or to stay comfortably at home doing nothing. The choice he makes, right there, determines how his life will unfold.

Oprah speaks about this often when she relates the story of watching her grandmother hanging laundry. Her grandmother told her, at age five or so, to pay attention so when Oprah became a maid herself, working for white people, she'd know what to do. Oprah could have chosen to take in that limiting belief. But even then, at that early age, she had an intuition that she was destined to do something more. And so the negative message did not take over and cause her to limit her beliefs.

The same thing is true of J. K. Rowling, who knew she had to be a writer, no matter what anyone else said. She had total belief in herself. She talks about "the one thing in my life that I believed—that I could tell a story."[143] Belief is the core.

Yet this is not everyone's experience. Think of the child who is brought up with a depressed or pessimistic parent, and who starts to believe the world really is as hopeless as the parent says it is. Such beliefs can be very hard to shift, even when they're not your own. The result is the same, though. The Soul sometimes simply cannot make itself heard above such self-talk. At some level, though, we all know if we're following our Souls or not. When we don't then a pervasive dissatisfaction infects and poisons much of what we do.

This is how the Unconscious not only ensures that we feel disappointed, but because we're not manifesting from the core of our being we feel it's only right that we feel bad about ourselves. That's because we have an inner sense of sadness that kicks in when we really aren't manifesting at our highest level. And that sense of unease seems to confirm the inner message that nothing good can happen. It truly is a desperate re-enforcing cycle. We cheat ourselves in the process.

Modern psychology and present-day therapists work with this sort of damage to the psyche every day. For the most part they urge their clients to have a slightly better notion of what the future may hold for them. That's a long way short of what your Soul has in mind. Your Soul wants you to revel in your life. Your Soul wants to heal fully.

Quite a few people, readers like you, will reach the end of this book and still be derailed by the wounded parts of your Unconscious self. Manifesting is not going to work under those circumstances. If you're aware of this danger, though, you can recognize that your

Soul is actually stronger than your history—if you decide to listen to what it says rather than tuning in to the past. It takes constant vigilance not to give in to these self-limiting beliefs. It requires us to stay open to possibilities all the time, and to listen to the voice of the Soul everywhere.

We have to live in the present, and we cannot afford "the luxury of a negative thought," as Louise Hay phrases it.[144]

The brutal truth is that we all have these negative beliefs in some measure. Almost everyone feels anxious before giving a public presentation. Behind that anxiety is the gnawing thought that perhaps we're not good enough to give this speech, raise this point, say what we feel. Whether it's a question of starting a business or telling a relative what we truly think, we all have those self-limiting beliefs, and each of us has our own set.

So, you may ask, what are your specific limiting beliefs? What keeps you from taking the steps you know you need to take? Well, you could spend a lot of time looking at them, and in the end you'd probably agree that they're strong—and then you'd most likely give in to them. It's not much use understanding what the problem is if you don't seek to change it. Take a different route. Trust your Soul. Believe it has something for you to do, and that you're good enough as a person to do it even if you don't do it perfectly. Especially if you don't do it perfectly. Believe that all your hurt has trained you for this purpose, to turn it to something positive. Then do it.

Belief, real belief, is the most powerful thing anyone can have, and with it, manifesting will always occur.

IN A NUTSHELL

1. Early conditioning tends to make us believe we're not good enough to have the life we want.

2. Overcoming such limiting beliefs is vital if we are to manifest the best life we can live.

3. Know what your limiting beliefs are. Heal them by transcending them.

Chapter 26
A Brief Recap of the Essentials of Manifesting

We will spell things out very simply here, to remind ourselves of how manifesting works at the highest level.

First: you have to know who you authentically are.

That means you have to be aware of your talents and treasure them, no matter how the rest of the world sees them. You'll also have to remember that the wounded parts of the ego will try to tell you things about yourself that are not true.

Second: you have to ask yourself how you can use your talents to help the world, using what you have to offer in joy.

Third: the best way to achieve #2 is to open your awareness and listen to your inner voice, to the voice of your Soul, and let that communication come through you.

Fourth: when you have an intuition about what you need to do, set the intention to do it. Then do it. Thoughts without actions will produce nothing.

Fifth: listen. You will be guided.

Sixth: stick with whatever it is you intend to do. Things take time and there are no short cuts.

PART SIX

Our Task Is to Manifest

Chapter 27
Why Are We Here?

If you already are a Soul, then what are we doing here in what Gary Zukav calls "the Earthschool"? Isn't it counter-productive to be stuck in a body? After all, if you've graduated from high school what's the point in going back and reliving the whole experience?

This question is actually not helpful, since there can never be a definite answer in the way we expect. Those who have had near-death experiences, like David Parsons (www.innercalling.org), Anita Moorjani, and Dr. Eben Alexander, are quite clear—they were sent back to our earth because they had a task to do. What the task is exactly they weren't told. They just know it has something to do with living a more conscious and loving life than before.

The short answer is that we can't know completely what our mission is because we're human. We have limited perceptions of what we do and the effects of our actions. We can't see very far into the future, if at all. Yet you can be absolutely sure that everything we do will have an effect on the future. We just have to know that we have a task to do and watch as it unfolds.

If we are to do this task, whatever it may be, then we'll have to be aligned with the power of Source. We'll need to be connected, in the only way we can be—by being our authentic selves and challenging our fears. Then we have to listen and act on what we feel we need to do. This requires us to trust that whatever it is we have to do will unveil itself. We are not here on earth to do things. We are here to have things done through us. We are not here to achieve things in the conventional sense. We are here to allow things to get done through us. Oprah phrases it slightly differently. She says that we are given gifts, and our task is to work out how we can give back as fully as possible.[145]

If this is true, then our questions to ourselves are probably going to be ones that ask how we can best serve the world. If you are a dancer, how can you best serve the world? Perhaps by inspiring others with your skills? Perhaps by teaching young dancers who will inspire still others? If you are an accountant, possibly your way to serve is by being the best accountant you can be and telling the truth about what you do. After all, we all can think of very fine accountants who used their genius to cook the financial statements of various Wall Street companies. If you are a home-maker, possibly the finest way you can serve is to help raise responsible children who feel loved and are loving. That would be a major contribution to our world. No task is to be taken for granted. We are all important.

The New Testament of the *Bible* can be very helpful here. St. John the Baptist went around preaching and baptizing people, but even as he did so he knew he was not the main event. He freely declared that there would be one who came after him who would be the real Messiah. It's a great metaphor for exactly what we've been considering. Not all of us can be the star turn, and that is perfectly fine. Knowing this is vitally important if we are to fulfill our destiny in the world. It's perfectly all right just to be who we feel ourselves authentically to be.

Here is Anita talking about the same subject:

Each of us is like a single thread in a huge tapestry woven in a complex and colorful pattern. We may be only one strand, yet we're all integral to the finished image.[146]

Gandhi famously expressed it this way: "It may seem impossible that what you are doing can make any difference at all; but it is vitally important you continue to do it!"

We are here to put our shoulders to the wheel. For when we serve others we are expressing love—and when we love, love comes back to us.

Maya Angelou had some wonderful insights into this. When she was asked at age 85 what she still wanted to achieve in her life, she made this remarkable and humble statement:

I've still not written as well as I want to write. I want to write so the reader in Des Moines, Iowa, in Kowloon, China, in Cape Town, Pretoria, South Africa, in Harlem, in Boston, I want to write so that that reader can say: "You know, that's the truth. I wasn't there and I wasn't a six feet tall black girl, but that's the truth. That's human."[147]

Revealing the truth, the deep truth that connects us all, was something she still longed to do even after all the books and poems she published. It was a loving and unending task, one that showed reverence for all people. It was not a task that ended when she became famous. It was a lifelong drive to keep doing what she was authentically called to do.

These statements are all remarkably similar in their views of what and who we are, and what we must do, since we are part of the oneness of the universe, and the universe needs us to be who we truly are so we can express love.

J. K. Rowling is perfectly clear that her Harry Potter stories are about "the redemptive power of love" and that every time there is conflict, "love wins."[148] This is simply because, "Love is the most powerful thing of all."[149] Anita Moorjani puts it this way: "This is pretty much all I have to do—just be the love I am, be who I am."[150] Oprah's entire career has been based in loving others and learning to love herself.

The bottom line is this: We are, unmistakably, here to love each other. When we do that we manifest the things that the world needs.

Chapter 28
How Can You Live a Magical Life?

———— ✦————✧————✦————

Let's reassure you right away—you already are living a magical life. Everything around you has been manifested by you. Once you realize this, the question shifts its shape. You always have lived a magical life, and what you see all around you is what you have chosen to manifest, whether you realize it or not.

The main thing for you to consider at this point is whether what you have manifested is what you feel comfortable with. Perhaps it is. Perhaps you look around your life, whatever it may be, and you see that it is one filled with love, with gratitude, and fulfillment. If you are in this space, it's worth remembering that nothing else matters. Money, possessions, fame—none of it matters as much as love and connectedness to others, and to the power that runs our universe. If you look around your world and feel discontent, and you sense that you are unconnected, then you'll have to set about manifesting what you do want; or to put it more accurately, you'll have to manifest what it is that your Soul tells you you need to do.

Remember—you're doing this manifesting all the time. Every second. Like breathing, you can choose how to breathe by noticing it. Do you draw short, nervous breaths? Or do you breathe easily and with free, grateful breaths? Is breathing a pleasure? Most of us simply do it, and don't think too much about it. Some of us gasp for breath out of nervousness or because we feel rushed. But we can choose. Like breathing, we are always connected to the Source, and our Souls stand willing to guide us to use the Source—but everyday things tend to get in the way, and we forget our spiritual nature in the rush of minor considerations that seem to run our lives. Anita expresses this beautifully: "Our sense of disconnection is simply part of the illusion of duality."[151] In other words, we don't have to choose between this and that, between what is spiritual and what is physical, because, actually, they are all part of the One. We just have to remind ourselves that we are never out of this connectedness. Once we see that we are always connected, even the ordinary facts of existence have their place.

This fits exactly with what we've been saying. You'll have noticed that you're not always manifesting at the highest level. Most of us don't—although saints probably do. Many of us don't manifest simply because we are choosing to focus our attention on things we want for selfish reasons, or for impossible reasons. Wanting a relative who is dying not to die is perhaps an example of this. Of course we don't want our relative or loved one to die! But sometimes this is what has to happen because the body cannot sustain the injuries it has received.

What we have to recognize is that if we change our attitude we will change the future in extraordinary ways. Ask anyone who has tearfully buried a loved one, and yet felt the love, and the meaning of that love, in a new way. Perhaps that was the lesson that was needed. A person's death has never been the end of anything. Sometimes it has permitted new recognitions, and an astonishing awareness of love that has lasted long after the funeral was over. In some instances the love simply couldn't be fully felt until the person had died, simply because of the weight of the past. We may have wanted the person to remain physically with us, but what we got was an eternal gift of the most valuable part of that person, one that lasts forever and gets passed on to everyone we meet. That's a magical gift. But we won't see it if we focus on the loss we feel.

The key to a magical life is to get back fully in tune with the universe, with a universe of powerful energy we've temporarily turned aside from, and reconnect with what it's nudging us towards. Usually that is about being more loving, more humane, more compassionate, more connected to others, and therefore to Source. This is Anita's take on this: "The energy flows through me, surrounds me, and is indistinguishable from me. It is, in fact, who and what I truly am."[152]

You'll find, of course, that even a magical life doesn't always go according to plan. You miss a train or a plane, or you don't get a job. You'll make mistakes and you find things work against you. It happens. Then you have to allow yourself to learn the lessons you were meant to learn. Perhaps missing that plane allowed you to feel more love for the person who was, unsuccessfully, trying to help you get there on time. Perhaps that opened another door for you, a door of wisdom and compassion. There's always a nugget of pure gold in there; always.

And we must always recall that we don't know the ultimate reasons that things happen the way they do. Think of Oprah and her audition for *The Color Purple*. If she'd got the part right away, the first time she tried, would she have learned that powerful lesson of surrender to the higher good? I doubt it. Surely she'd have got the lesson later in life, but it was vitally important that she should have that specific lesson at that specific time—and it transformed who she is and what she does.

This is what we mean when we say "the universe will support you."

It will provide exactly what you need in order to grow spiritually and to stay present to your Soul, and it will not let you down.

The universe won't change your life overnight without your effort—instead it will give you the openings so that you can change your life, so you can become the best version of yourself that is possible. It will give you many opportunities to grow spiritually. And it does this so you can grow stronger. The universe requires your participation, just as any exercise or diet program does, and that participation expects you to change your mindset about who you are and what you can do. If you want to lose ten pounds, you have to take action and believe it's possible. If you want to bring love into your life, fully, you have to do the same thing.

If you aim to manifest love and abundance, you can start any time you wish. The universe has been waiting for you to make that decision, and it will greet you with open arms. You are already living a magical life.

Chapter 29
The Highest Form of Abundance

By now I think you will have a good idea about what this abundance may look like, but there's always a benefit in spelling things out. The highest form of abundance comes directly to you from the limitless energy of a universe that is constantly creating stars, galaxies, and everything else, ceaselessly. This abundance comes to you because you have aligned with your Soul and listened to your Soul's intentions. It's like plugging in to a light socket of boundless energy.

When we do this the abundance arrives in our hands because we have shown that we know how it can be used. It appears because we've shown we know what it's for and we have some good notions for making it useful, now and into the future. Abundance does occasionally arrive for those who have no idea how to use it, and the result is almost always misery for them—you've only to think of those who inherit enormous wealth and who then squander it to know what that looks like.

The abundant wealth of the universe arrives in many forms. It may appear as a series of seemingly miraculous contacts with the right people, who can help you to fulfill your purpose. It may appear as a "new-found" talent such as artistic or personal expression, or the ability to persuade others. It may appear as a loving partner or a group of people who will be instrumental in helping you all bring out the very best in each other. Often it comes in the form of a child who can transform the lives of all who are around him or her. Sometimes it appears as money, which can help make things happen, or wealth of another measurable kind. Sometimes it appears as a lightness of spirit and an inner joy that inspires others, even as it raises the person who receives it to higher spiritual awareness.

Ideally we may be lucky enough to manifest all these attributes. But if we don't, then there is no blame attached. Perhaps it means there may be a few more spiritual lessons to learn as we help to contribute to the evolving consciousness of our planet as a whole. Or perhaps it means that the individual's Soul purpose is being served right now in exactly in the way it needs to be, and that a more modest situation is perfect for what is evolving. After all, if we all manifested wealth and a mansion in Hawaii there would be no one living in less exalted places, quietly meeting and inspiring others who live in more modest surroundings. The universe does not want to isolate the effective manifesters on an island where they only have each other to talk to.

When we see a person who is in the space of genuine abundance, we become aware that this individual is so closely aligned with his or her Soul intention that it feels seamless, effortless. This person seems to be wise in unexpected ways, since he or she will be able to see the deep motivations of others, understanding them and not judging but accepting them. At times it may feel as if the person has achieved such authentic power that he or she can read minds. The loving Soul is very often so attuned to the emotions and needs of others that it can seem uncanny to those who feel themselves laid bare by the level of compassionate understanding they receive. The authentically empowered person operates deliberately and without hesitation, doing what is right and loving, and trusting fully in the intuitive messages that come every day from the Soul. There is no gap between intention and action. Instead there is a deep joy, one that can be noticed by others. This is a person who is living fully from the Soul, because that is what happens when we tap into the energy of the universe—the Soul grows and uses us as a powerful organ of expression. It becomes more fully what it was always capable of being. In fact the loving, compassionate Soul cannot achieve its full power until we are connected in this way. The individual then becomes the earthly expression of the Soul's power channeled to it. We see this as harmony, as a person who is not at war with himself or anyone or anything. This is a peacemaker. This person is an earthly expression of the loving power of the universe, sent to inspire, and to heal the discords of others.

How does this work? In the documentary movie *Fierce Grace* (2000) spiritual seeker Ram Dass goes to see Neem Karoli Baba, a guru in India, and immediately feels totally understood by this person, at peace and accepted and as if the man knows all his thoughts. The guru is then described in a very interesting way when one of the interviewees says that it wasn't as if you felt loved by the guru when you were in his presence, so much as that you felt that everyone else in the room was suddenly much more loving of each other. Nothing else felt more important, he says. What a wonderful experience that must have been, and what a lesson to us all.

It is exactly this lesson that is at the core of Oprah's loving, caring desire to raise awareness. It is at the core of J. K. Rowling's novels, in which love is always the strongest force. And it is in Anita Moorjani's books and public speaking, which let us know that we have to love others and ourselves in order to make our connection to the Source. It's the same message.

The highest abundance comes to us through a truly loving awareness, like a doorway opening to the eternal love of the universe.

Afterword

We chose to focus this book on three women who manifested lives that went beyond even their expectations. We could have chosen 30, or perhaps 130, if we'd been interested in proving something by way of statistics. But this isn't about statistics. After all, if you want to be a great athlete you don't interview 5,000 mediocre athletes. You interview only the very best.

Another advantage of choosing just three people is that they remain memorable people for the reader, whereas more examples would just become confusing. We chose Oprah, J. K. Rowling, and Anita Moorjani because by focusing on them we can get a clearer picture of what they're doing so that we can convey it to you. Inevitably with three people whose lives are so similar you will find a fair amount of repetition. That's not bad; it is through repetition that we learn best.

You'll have noticed that these three very different public figures have been extraordinarily open about how their lives unfolded, about how they manifested their lives. Almost all the information in this book comes from public sources—things they have said or written in interviews, articles, and books about their lives. These are statements they have deliberately chosen to share with others. There's no "insider track" here, no special secret they revealed only in the privacy of a closed interview. They want you to know this information!

What we discovered is that all three—and all the other people we've used as examples—say almost exactly the same thing: the way to manifest a fulfilled and extraordinary life is to work with the true intentions of your Soul, and that it is by opening yourself to the whisper of your Higher Awareness that you can achieve this.

Notes

1. J. K. Rowling, *Very Good Lives: The Fringe Benefits of Failure and the Importance of Imagination,* Little, Brown and Company, 2015.

2. "Oprah Winfrey, The Story of the Most Successful Black Woman of All Time." *E! True Hollywood Story,* 26 December 2012.

3. *The Oprah Winfrey Show,* 3 April 2011.

4. Oprah Winfrey, O, The Oprah Magazine, November 2010.

5. Marianne Williamson, 20 February 2013. https:// www. facebook.com/207697880579/posts/i-love-this-one-as-reported-by-wayne-dyermany-years-ago-oprah-winfrey-was-interv/10152542100765580

6. *J. K. Rowling: A Year in the Life.* Television documentary, ITV, 2007.

7. Decca Aitkenhead, "J. K. Rowling: 'The Worst That Can Happen Is That Everyone Says, That's Shockingly Bad'," Guardian, 22 September 2012.

8. *J. K. Rowling: A Year in the Life.*

9. *J. K. Rowling: A Year in the Life.*

10. Anita Moorjani, *Dying to Be Me: My Journey from Cancer, to Near Death, to True Healing,* Hay House, 2012. p. 76.

11. "The Greatest Discovery of Oprah's Life," Oprah.com, May 2008. https:// www.oprah.com/spirit/the-greatest-discovery-of-oprahs-life

12. J. K. Rowling, Very Good Lives.

13. Gary Zukav, *The Seat of the Soul,* Rider, 2015.

14. *Super Soul Sunday,* 24 February 2013.

15. Gary Zukav, *The Seat of the Soul.*

16. *Super Soul Sunday,* 24 February 2013.

17. Moorjani, *Dying to Be Me,* p. 113.

18. Moorjani, *Dying to Be Me,* p. 113.

19. Moorjani, *Dying to Be Me,* pp. 120–1.

20. "Oprah & Eben Alexander," *Super Soul Sunday,* OWN, 12 December 2012.

21. "Oprah & Eben Alexander," *Super Soul Sunday.*

22. Cragg, Michael, "New music extra: George Michael—White Light," Guardian, 30 June 2012.

23. www.nderf.org

24. Susy Macaulay. "J. K. Rowling: Why boy wizard Harry Potter and Arbroath will forever be linked," The Courier, 17 December 2021. https://www.thecourier.co.uk/fp/past-times/2831583/harry-potter-arbroath

25. *J.K. Rowling: A Year in the Life.*

26. *J.K. Rowling: A Year in the Life.*

27. Oprah's Master Class, season 2, episode 8, 3 April 2011.

28. Oprah's Master Class, season 2, episode 8, 3 April 2011.

29. Oprah's Master Class, season 2, episode 8, 3 April 2011.

30. Bloomberg Game Changers: "J.K. Rowling." 31 May 2011.

31. Decca Aitkenhead, "J. K. Rowling: 'The Worst That Can Happen . . .'"

32. Moorjani, *Dying to Be Me,* p. 138.

33. Moorjani, *Dying to Be Me,* p. 139.

34. Wallace Stevens, "Peter Quince at the Clavier," Harmonium, Dover Publications, Inc, 2019.

35. Moorjani, *Dying to Be Me,* p. 153.

36 . Decca Aitkenhead, "J. K. Rowling: 'The Worst That Can Happen . . .'"

37. Moorjani, *Dying to Be Me,* p. 144.

38. Moorjani, *Dying to Be Me,* p. 137.

39. Moorjani, *Dying to Be Me,* p. 137.

40. *The Oprah Winfrey Show,* 3 April 2011.

41. *J. K. Rowling: A Year in the Life.*

42. Oprah Winfrey, "What Oprah Knows for Sure About Destiny." Oprah.com, https://www.oprah.com/inspiration/what-oprah-knows-for-sure-about-destiny.

43. Oprah Winfrey, "What Oprah Knows for Sure About Destiny."

44. Oprah Winfrey, "What Oprah Knows for Sure About Destiny."

45. Oprah Winfrey, "What Oprah Knows for Sure About Destiny."

46. Oprah Winfrey, "What Oprah Knows for Sure About Destiny."

47. Decca Aitkenhead, "J. K. Rowling: 'The Worst That Can Happen . . .'"

48. Gary Zukav, *The Seat of the Soul.*

49. Oprah's Master Class, OWN, 16 January 2011.

50. Oprah's Master Class, OWN, 27 March 2011.

51. Oprah's Master Class, OWN, 27 March 2011.

52. Wallace D. Wattles, *The Science of Getting Rich,* Outskirts Press, 2009.

53. https://www.goodreads.com/quotes/8745896-when-heaven-is-about-to-confer-a-great-responsibility-on

54. Moorjani, *Dying to Be Me,* p. 157.

55. Moorjani, *Dying to Be Me,* p. 157.

56. Moorjani, *Dying to Be Me,* p. 158.

57. *J. K. Rowling: A Year in the Life.*

58. Forbes, Moira, "Oprah Winfrey Talks Philanthropy, Failure And What Every Guest—Including Beyoncé—Asks Her," *Forbes Magazine*, 18 September 2012, https://www.forbes.com/sites/ moiraforbes/2012/09/18/oprah-winfrey-talks-philanthropy- failure-and-what-every-guest-including-beyonce-asks-her

59. Oprah Winfrey's 2008 Stanford Commencement Address, Stanford, 15 June 2008. https://www.youtube.com/ watch?v=Bpd3raj8xww

60. Forbes, Moira, "Oprah Winfrey Talks Philanthropy . . ."

61. Forbes, Moira, "Oprah Winfrey Talks Philanthropy . . ."

62. Oprah Winfrey, "The Story of the Most Successful Black Woman of All Time," *E! True Hollywood Story*, 26 December 2012.

63. Oprah Winfrey, "Most Successful Black Woman."

64. Forbes, Moira, "Oprah Winfrey Talks Philanthropy . . ."

65. Oprah Winfrey, "The Story of the Most Successful Black Woman of All Time."

66. "Oprah & Gary Zukav," *Super Soul Sunday*, OWN, 14 July 2013.

67. "Oprah & Gary Zukav," *Super Soul Sunday*.

68. "Oprah & Gary Zukav," *Super Soul Sunday*.

69. "Oprah & Gary Zukav," *Super Soul Sunday*.

70. Gary Zukav, *The Seat of the Soul*.

71. Gary Zukav, *The Seat of the Soul*.

72. Gary Zukav, *The Seat of the Soul*.

73. "Oprah & Gary Zukav," *Super Soul Sunday*, OWN, 14 July 2013.

74. Leonard Cohen, "Going Home," Old Ideas, 2012.

75. Oprah's Master Class, OWN, z.d. https://www.youtube.com/ watch?v=S-skrmHCoiRc

76. Oprah's Master Class, OWN.

77. *The Oprah Winfrey Show*, 1 October 2010, https://www.youtube.com/watch?v=gTotbiUjLxw

78. *The Oprah Winfrey Show*, 1 October 2010.

79. Moorjani, *Dying to Be Me*, p. 158.

80. Moorjani, *Dying to Be Me*, p. 159.

81. Moorjani, *Dying to Be Me*, p. 159.

82. Moorjani, *Dying to Be Me*, p. 148.

83. "'My Women Heroes': The Powerful Lesson Maya Angelou Taught Oprah." Oprah's Lifeclass, OWN, 20 October 2011, https://www.youtube.com/watch?v=fx447ShQLeE

84 / 85. "Understanding Spiritual Partnerships in Your Life," *Super Soul Sunday*, OWN, 12 February 2012.

86. "Dr. Maya Angelou's Advice for Oprah in Her Darkest Moments," *The Oprah Winfrey Show*, OWN, z.d. https://www.youtube.com/watch?v=lxz- rM7OFK6U

87. Derrick Bryson Taylor, "Oprah Shares a Lesson Dr. Maya Angelou Taught Her," Essence, 28 October 2020.

88. "The Powerful Lesson Maya Angelou Taught Oprah," Oprah's Lifeclass, OWN, 20 October 2011 https://www.youtube.com/watch?v=fx447ShQLeE

89. Moorjani, *Dying to Be Me*, p. 128.

90. Oprah's Master Class, season 2, episode 8, 3 April 2011.

91. Oprah's Master Class, season 2, episode 8, 3 April 2011.

92. Oprah's Master Class, season 2, episode 8, 3 April 2011.

93. Oprah's Master Class, season 2, episode 8, 3 April 2011.

94. Moorjani, *Dying to Be Me*, p. 137.

95. "Jim Carrey on 'Awakening,'" Eckhart Tolle TV, https://www.youtube.com/watch?v=uIaY0l5qV0c

96. Frank Golbig, personal interview with Dr. Allan Hunter, 10 February 2000.

97. Moorjani, *Dying to Be Me,* p. 155.

98. Moorjani, *Dying to Be Me,* p. 155.

99. Moorjani, *Dying to Be Me,* p. 115.

100. Moorjani, *Dying to Be Me,* p. 161.

101. Moorjani, *Dying to Be Me,* p. 161.

102. Moorjani, *Dying to Be Me,* p. 137.

103. *The Oprah Winfrey Show,* 1 October 2010, https://www.youtube.com/watch?v=gTotbiUjLxw

104. *The Oprah Winfrey Show,* 1 October 2010.

105. Oprah.com, "The Brilliant Mind Behind Harry Potter," October 2010.

106. Interview with Baptist de Pape about *The Power of the Heart,* Kosmos Uitgevers, 2014.

107. Interview with Baptist de Pape about *The Power of the Heart.*

108 Interview with Baptist de Pape about *The Power of the Heart.*

109. "Oprah & Sarah Ban Breathnach," *Super Soul Sunday,* OWN, 10 June 2012.

110. "Oprah & Sarah Ban Breathnach," *Super Soul Sunday.*

111. Personal conversation with Baptist de Pape, British Colombia, Canada, 2012.

112. Oprah's Master Class, part 2, 4 April 2011.

113. Oprah's Master Class, part 2, 4 April 2011.

114. "Why Oprah Decided to Start Her OWN Network," Oprah.com, January 2011 https://www.oprah.com/spirit/oprah-winfrey-network-sneak-preview#ixz-z23oQWzvBD

115. "Why Oprah Decided to Start Her OWN Network."

116. "Why Oprah Decided to Start Her OWN Network."

117. "Why Oprah Decided to Start Her OWN Network."

118. Interview by Baptist de Pape about *The Power of the Heart*, Kosmos Uitgevers, 2014.

119. "Oprah & India Arie," *Super Soul Sunday*, OWN, 23 June 2013.

120. "Oprah & India Arie," *Super Soul Sunday*.

121. Winfrey, Oprah, "The Power of Real," Oprah.com, October 2010, https://www.oprah.com/spirit/oprah-on-the-importance-of-authenticity-what-i-know-for-sure

122. "Oprah & India Arie," *Super Soul Sunday*, OWN, 23 June 2013.

123. "Oprah & India Arie," *Super Soul Sunday*.

124. "Oprah & India Arie," *Super Soul Sunday*.

125. Winfrey, Oprah, "The Power of Real," Oprah.com, October 2010, https://www.oprah.com/spirit/oprah-on-the-importance-of-authenticity-what-i-know-for-sure

126. "Oprah & India Arie," *Super Soul Sunday*, OWN, 23 June 2013.

127. "Oprah & India Arie," *Super Soul Sunday*.

128. Podrazik, Joan, "India Arie's Definition of Success," Huffpost.com, 29.

129. "Oprah & India Arie," *Super Soul Sunday*, OWN, 23 June 2013.

130. "Oprah & India Arie," *Super Soul Sunday*.

131. Phillips, Max, "The Definition of Success You Need to Understand for 10x More Clarity," Medium.com, 13 September 2020. https://medium.com/the-ascent/the-definition-of-success-you-need-to-understand-for-10x-more-clarity-6cd245834ed1

132. Interview with Baptist de Pape for *The Power of the Heart*, Kosmos Uitgevers, 2014.

133. Interview with Baptist de Pape for *The Power of the Heart*.

134. Interview with Baptist de Pape for *The Power of the Heart*.

135. Fisher, Luchina, "Ups and Downs of the Oprah Winfrey Network," ABC News, 4 February 2013. https://abcnews.go.com/Entertainment/ups-downs-oprah-winfrey-network/story?id=18401567

136. *Watch What Happens Live*, Bravo TV, 16 August 2013.

137. *Watch What Happens Live*, Bravo TV.

138. *Watch What Happens Live*, Bravo TV.

139. Kevin Dolak, "Ups and Downs of the Oprah Winfrey Network," ABC News, 16 July 2012. https://abcnews.go.com/Entertainment/oprah-win-frey-reveals-struggles-network/story?id=16784944

140. Dolak, "Ups and Downs of the Oprah Winfrey Network."

141 *Watch What Happens Live*, Bravo TV, 16 August 2013.

142. *Watch What Happens Live*, Bravo TV.

143. *Watch What Happens Live*, Bravo TV.

144. Quoted in: McWilliams, Peter, You Can't Afford The Luxury Of A Negative Thought, Prelude Press, 1995.

145. Oprah's Lifeclass, OWN, 5 July, 2013 and 1 October 2010.

146. Moorjani, *Dying to Be Me*, p. 151.

147. Belinda Luscombe, "10 Questions With Maya Angelou," 8 April 2013. https://time.com/123087/10-questions-with-maya-angelou

148. *J. K. Rowling: A Year in the Life.*

149. *J. K. Rowling: A Year in the Life.*

150. Moorjani, *Dying to Be Me*, p. 150.

151. Moorjani, *Dying to Be Me*, p. 116.

152. Moorjani, *Dying to Be Me*, p. 128.

Index

About the Author

Photo by Verellen Photography

Baptist de Pape is a lawyer turned author and filmmaker, known for his book and documentary *The Power of the Heart* (Atria Books / Simon & Schuster) which was published in more than 80 countries.

Mired in anxiety and fears about his future, de Pape felt the call to investigate the incredible power of the heart and how it can lead us to our true purpose in life. On a quest that took him around the world, he interviewed eighteen living icons—all on camera—including Isabel Allende, Jane Goodall, Paulo Coelho, Deepak Chopra, Eckhart Tolle, and Maya Angelou. Generously sharing their touching personal stories as well as profound guidance, these leaders co-created with de Pape a multidimensional, illuminating portrait of the heart as an inexhaustible source of love and wisdom that far surpasses that of the mind. The findings of this journey inspired him not only to create *The Power of the Heart* but also to investigate what it is that has people overcome obstacles in life, make them resilient, and enable them to manifest the life they desire. *Manifestation Perfected* is the result of this research. Baptist de Pape lives in Belgium.

For more information visit:

Instagram: **baptistdepapeofficial**

website: **thepoweroftheheart.com**

Facebook: **Baptist de Pape**